MOUSEL.

ON YOUR OWN

GEOFFREY CROFT

BROOKE SHIELDS

ON YOUR OWN

 Villard Books   New York 1985

Photographs by Oliviero Toscani, Paul Amato, Denis Piel,
are reproduced courtesy of *Vogue:*
copyright © 1981, 1983 and 1984 by The Condé Nast Publications Inc.
Photographs by Jacques Malignon and Renato Grignaschi
are reproduced courtesy of *Bride's*
© 1983 and 1984 by The Condé Nast Publications Inc.

LIBRARY OF CONGRESS CATALOGING IN PUBLICATION DATA
Shields, Brooke, 1965–
On your own.
1. Women college students—United States—Life skills
guides. 2. College student orientation—United States.
I. Title.
LC1757.S54   1985   378'.198   84-40606
ISBN 0-394-54460-9

Designed by Helen Barrow
Manufactured in the United States of America
9 8 7 6 5 4 3 2
First Edition

I dedicate this book to you.
It is my way of giving something to everyone
who has ever supported and encouraged me.

ACKNOWLEDGMENTS

I am, of course, grateful to all the photographers whose work appears in these pages, but especially to Patrick Demarchelier for contributing so much of his time to this book. And to Robert Risko for his delightful illustrations.

Special thanks to Al Lowman, Diane Reverand, Wendy Bass, and Patricia Barlow for their artistic guidance, enthusiasm, and belief in this book.

Without the help of my aunt, Lila Wisdom, the whole process would not have gone as smoothly.

And, most of all, my mother, Teri Shields, deserves my deepest gratitude for the love and support she has unselfishly given me all my life.

Contents

ON YOUR OWN

FRANKIE ZITHS © 1983

Introduction

So FAR I've led a glamorous and exciting life—one filled with rare opportunities. I'm grateful that I've traveled all over the world, have met so many interesting people, and have had a wonderful and fulfilling career. Behind all the trappings of celebrity, I am a young woman making my way through college, learning to be independent and to take responsibility for myself.

Like anyone else, I've had to grow up and take those big steps away from home. Some of us can't wait to leave. Many find that the grown-up world isn't everything that we thought it would be. If you're like me, you're playing it safe, inching your way out the door until your parents give you that final push.

Making the transition from dependent child to young adult is not always easy. It can be a time of rebellion and hurt feelings. One moment you're struggling to break away and the next moment you're clinging to your childhood for dear life. As much as you want your freedom, your independence, you're not always prepared to accept the necessary adjustments. Friends are no longer just playmates. They become advisors who provide you with an emotional support system as you face the problems of the adult world together. Along with your new freedom, boyfriends can become more demanding, expecting something more serious than a good-night kiss, often more of you than you're ready to give. And when it comes to your parents, your relationship may have to be redefined while you continue to give them the respect they deserve.

In the midst of all of this emotional turmoil, so much is expected of you. Sometimes, as you're adjusting to these life changes, it's easy to let things slide—your health and nutritional needs, your exercise program, and your looks. No matter how crazy or chaotic your life seems, these are basics that must be maintained and balanced for the rest of your life.

Every day you're confronted with new challenges as you learn, explore, expand, and absorb as much as you possibly can to prepare yourself for the future. The pressure is on to achieve good grades and to choose a career. As you struggle to find your place in the world, many of your old values are discarded as you establish new ones. This is your time to recognize your individuality and to determine what's right for you.

Shaping and maintaining your beliefs and values can be difficult when confronting peer pressure. Every new friend you make has something different to share. Everybody has advice about what you should do—boyfriends say one thing, girlfriends something else. And of course there are your parents' beliefs to consider. Regardless of who is telling you what, you have to make your own decisions. I know that being on my own means that I have to take responsibility for my actions. There are no easy outs. I must be prepared to deal with the consequences of whatever choices I make in an adult way.

Ultimately, being on your own is about finding balance in your life. You've got to be involved with people and activities, be open to new ideas, and at the same time maintain a sense of yourself. You can be sensitive to others and remain true to yourself. This is the time to focus on yourself, nurture and define yourself, but don't become so self-indulgent that you miss what's going on around you or that you stop growing.

Test, try, experiment, take a chance—but try to think things through before you act. And don't be afraid to make a mistake, because very little is irreversible. Don't get stuck in situations you really don't like—whether it involves a jealous boyfriend, messy roommate, or choice of major. Don't be afraid to make a change. What's important is that you always feel good about yourself regardless of what you do.

In writing *On Your Own,* I wanted to share what I've learned through the trials and errors of my own experiences. So this book is a little bit Brooke—from my innermost worries and dreams to my unique relationship with my mother—and lots of "how to's" that I've picked up along the way. I'll give you tips on your college wardrobe, my favorite makeup tricks, study hints, and of course the opposite sex—I'll even help you deal with your parents. As you'll read, my terrific experiences have been balanced by those that were confusing and sad. There are times when I get as upset and hysterical as any other young adult—times when I just don't know what to do. But I take heart in knowing that we all have our problems as we come of age, that I'm not alone.

Despite the problems, this is a wonderful time in my life. I love becoming an adult and I'm adjusting to making all the choices and decisions that come with this new role. No, it isn't easy, but I think you will find it exhilarating to realize that you're capable of taking charge of every aspect of your life and making good choices on your own. I know that you'll love the feeling of self-respect that comes with controlling your own life and having the power to achieve success and create your happiness—on your own.

BROOKE SHIELDS
January 1985

GEOFFREY CROFT

Taking a lunch break with my friend Cecelie Astrup.

Health and Nutrition

I WAS a prime rib and steak girl until I turned thirteen and became enlightened. I choose to be a modified vegetarian (I still eat fish and eggs) because this is the diet that works for me. I don't profess that my way is right for everybody, and since I'm not a doctor or nutritionist I would not presume to suggest a specific diet for you. I believe what you put inside is going to show outside—which is why you should make it an urgent priority to find a diet customized for your needs.

Over the years most of us have depended on "Mom" to provide us with healthy, well-balanced meals. But once you're on your own, it's up to you to make the right food choices. Often it's difficult to maintain a good diet at college because there are so many temptations, and no one around to tell you "No!" And don't overlook the wonders of institutional food. Soggy vegetables and an overabundance of carbos can make sane eating very difficult. Coping with dining hall smorgasbords takes real discipline. If you're living in an apartment and cooking for yourself, mealtime may be such a bother that you take the easy way out: JUNK FOOD!

One of the major adjustments to being on your own is taking responsibility for your eating habits. Now is the time for you to discover the diet that's right for you, a diet that controls your weight, gives you shiny hair and healthy skin, makes you feel good, and provides you with the necessary energy to get you through the day.

ROBERT RISKO

The "right diet" doesn't leave you feeling deprived or obsessed by food, and even permits the occasional splurges that come with holidays and celebrations.

Food should never be a source of frustration, regardless of how strict your diet must be. I certainly can sympathize with anyone who becomes overwhelmed by the entire dieting package—calories, carbohydrates, weight control, health food versus junk food, ad infinitum. Hearing "You are what you eat" might make you want to explode—or even worse, binge. After all, you might say to yourself, I wouldn't mind being a chocolate chip cookie.

I know that if I didn't love to eat, my life would definitely be easier. Not only do I have to diet constantly to keep my weight down, but I also have to deal with food allergies. I'm allergic to tomatoes, potatoes, malt, sugar, and all dairy products. The reactions I have to these foods vary from an uncomfortable fullness—as in bloat—to a warm itchy feeling on a red face. As you can imagine, my diet is very limited. If I want to feel and look good, I have to accept and cope with these limitations as best I can.

Mainly, my diet consists of fish (I love sushi!), tofu, nuts and raisins, eggs, soy milk, granola, fruits, vegetables, salads, and rice cakes. Although restricted, my diet is a balance of protein, carbohydrates, and minimal fats. It provides me with loads of energy, and allows me to control my weight as long as I limit my portions. Like all of us, I occasionally can't resist something that I know I should, or I really go overboard and pig-out for a meal. But I survive these splurges by going right back on my diet the next day. I've learned through experience that consistency is the secret to successful dieting.

Finding Your Diet

I've always been *food aware,* and have been fine-tuning my diet since I was eight years old. It began with soda and pizza. After school my girl-friends and I always had the same snack until I heard that a certain carbonated beverage could take the paint off a car. Since I don't have a cast-iron stomach, I was distressed to imagine what it was doing to me. I decided to give it up and to drink water or juice instead. After abstaining for two weeks, I couldn't believe how awful and sweet a glass of cola tasted to me. I knew that I was definitely better off without it.

A few years later, when being a vegetarian sounded interesting and the toxicity of meat was being publicized, I decided to test my reaction to meat. I gave it up for a week and was amazed at how energetic I felt without it. Considering my newfound energy and all the calories that I would be saving, I decided to give it up permanently. A couple of years later I was curious to see what would happen if I ate meat again. I didn't get ill or have stomach cramps—but it made me feel strange and very, very sluggish. I knew that being a modified vegetarian was right for me—I need all the energy that I can get.

Since our bodies respond to food so differently, it is important to find a diet that suits our individual needs. Little did I know, when I first started testing foods, that my dietary needs would be determined by my food allergies.

Food allergies can be sneaky—you suddenly feel rotten but you don't know why. Or maybe you feel flushed, queasy, have a headache or stomach cramps after you eat certain foods. Food allergies can provoke a wide range of symptoms, some of them very subtle, and are now being linked to obesity and compulsive eating. Believe it or not, you can actually crave and become addicted to the very foods that you're allergic to! So if you suspect that you're a victim of food allergies, talk to your doctor about getting tested. Now, by just taking a sample of your blood, he can quickly test a broad range of foods. Once you find out what foods you're allergic to, you simply eliminate them from your diet and create a balanced diet from the foods you're not allergic to. Eliminating problem foods will make you feel better, help you lose weight, and ultimately make you look better too.

The best way to lose weight is to count your calories and carbohydrates. If you keep your calorie count to 1000 calories/day and your carbohydrates to 60 carbs/day you will lose 1–3 pounds a week depending on your activity level, or "activity factor." Once you reach your ideal weight, the number of calories you need to maintain that weight is determined by this activity factor. To find your activity factor use this standard formula:

❧ If you sit most of the day and do no regular exercise, your activity factor is 12.

❧ If you spend several hours a day on your feet, walking, lightly exercising, your activity factor is 13.

❧ If you're extremely active, spending many hours a day doing physical labor or working out strenuously, your activity factor is 15.

By multiplying your activity factor by your ideal weight, you will get an estimate of the number of calories you can eat.

When you lose weight slowly and sensibly, and work to maintain your ideal weight, your eating habits improve and your body stabilizes. Crash dieting yo-yos your system, doesn't do anything for your eating habits, and often leaves you feeling weak. If you want to lose more, exercise more. Combining a sensible diet with lots of exercise is the most efficient way to lose weight and to keep it off. By avoiding starvation diets, you won't feel deprived and your energy level stays high.

Now for a list of my own Diet Do's and Don'ts that have always helped me to keep my weight under control:

- A daily multivitamin should be taken to make sure your daily nutritional needs are covered.
- Drink lots of water, as much as you can. Eight glasses a day is the minimum. It fills you up, flushes out your system, and works internally to keep your skin moist and soft.
- Purchase a pocket-size calorie/carbohydrate counter and use it!
- If you're really on a strict weight loss diet, try not to eat after 6 o'clock. If you must, have an apple or a cup of unbuttered popcorn.
- Fruit juices are higher in calories, so limit your intake and load up on pure vegetable juices instead.
- Better yet, fill yourself up with as many crunchy, raw vegetables as you can stand. You can never eat too many.
- A nice crunchy apple is a dieter's treat food that I absolutely love.
- Eat half a grapefruit or even peel it like an orange and drink a glass of warm lemon water (which helps keep you regular) one-half hour before meals. This way you won't be ravenous when you get to the dining hall, tempted to eat everything in sight.
- Cut your normal portions in half.
- Don't skip meals. Otherwise you'll get too hungry and over-compensate at the next meal.
- Remember: Balance, balance, balance!

Dealing with Your Diet

Once you develop your diet, you've got to naturalize it so you can follow it daily without fuss and embarrassment. What could be more boring than someone who spends hours talking about her diet? All that complaining is so unattractive. Just remember that nobody wants to hear about the details of your diet, your failures and triumphs, so don't talk it to death. Just follow it with quiet resolve. Your diet is *your* diet. Nobody else cares.

You don't have to live like a hermit just because you're following a special diet. As strict as my diet is, I can always find something to eat when I go out. In almost every restaurant, a health salad is always available. Even if it's not on the menu, it won't hurt to ask. Since I don't use creamy dressings, I mix my own oil, vinegar, and mustard dressing right at the table. I skip the bread and soup and order some nice broiled fish with lemon. Or maybe I'll just order a plate of steamed vegetables. A couple of drops of soy sauce really adds flavor.

It's easy to have a balanced meal at a restaurant that doesn't wreck your diet, but you have to approach the situation with the right attitude. If you look at your friend's plate and start drooling, you're going to be miserable. Making woeful comments like, "This is all I can have," "I wish I could eat what you're eating," or "Gosh, these vegetables are boring," will only draw attention to the fact that you're on a diet. What girl in her right mind wants her date to know that she has to diet?

If I'm having dinner at a friend's house, I quietly help myself to what I can eat. Once again, a salad and vegetable is almost always served. If something special has been prepared that's not on my diet, I make sure to taste it and to compliment the cook. By not drawing attention to what I'm choosing to eat, people rarely notice how careful I am about my diet. People are always saying, "Oh, you. You never have to diet." Little do they know.

Avoiding Dining Hall Disaster

A meal is a break from work, a wonderful social time. I love going to the dining hall or my club to have a meal with my friends. Sometimes it's our only chance to get caught up on all the good gossip. Unfortunately, it's tempting to eat everything in sight—especially when you feel as if you have only three chances each day to stoke it in! But you've got to remember that the dining hall is for survival eating, *not* pigging out. Continual overindulgence can cause those extra pounds, known as the "freshman fifteen," to start creeping on.

Luckily, at Princeton we have a vegetarian section in the dining hall. I avoided "freshman fifteen" during my first year of college by fo-

GEOFFREY CROFT

cusing on the salad bar, vegetables, and fish whenever it was available. I avoided ice cream, potatoes, and bread. If I had to have dessert, I made sure I grabbed a piece of fruit.

Let's face it—the only way to avoid dining hall disaster and the resulting "freshman fifteen" is to discipline yourself by sticking to your diet no matter what. You might want to consider these dining hall diversionary tactics:

- In the back of your mind, at all times, should be the image of yourself in a bathing suit at some hot spot during spring break, where the last thing you'll want to look like is an overweight college girl.
- Pretend that you're at home and that the pantry and fridge are stocked with healthy, low-calorie foods. Everything else you see is a mirage created by too much studying.
- Pretend that your mother is in the corner watching every bite you take and that she's sitting next to a big scale.
- What you can't fit on your tray, you can't have.
- Never go back for seconds, it's too tempting!
- Don't put anything on your tray that you don't need nutritionally.
- Eat slowly and talk to your friends. You'll fill up faster, be distracted from all the food around you and probably swallow a lot of air.
- Have a close friend take a Polaroid of you in a bathing suit and put it somewhere that only you will see it—for example, the first page of your notebook or the refrigerator door. Just make sure that you see it often.
- If you find yourself gaining the "freshman fifteen" *plus,* cancel your dining hall contract for a semester and invest in a small refrigerator, blender, and hot plate (if allowed). Swear to yourself that you'll keep only healthy, low-cal foods in the refrigerator. You'll need the blender for your diet drinks, not milkshakes or daiquiris, and the hot plate for boiling water for all those hard-boiled eggs you'll be eating.

Dealing with the Reality of Pizza and Ice Cream and Coping with Late Night Snacks

Believe it or not, if you behave yourself in the dining hall and stick to your diet, you can indulge in an occasional slice of pizza or dish of ice cream and still stay thin. Just remember that the key is moderation—this means eating one slice of pizza, not half a pie, and having a single scoop of ice cream and not a sloppy sundae. But even in moderation, pizza and sweets cannot be consumed every night unless you don't mind *wearing* the consequences.

I try to avoid eating late night snacks because the calories just don't burn up while you sleep. It's hard not to munch while studying—I get so hungry. If I'm studying late at night, I'll eat some carrots, celery, or an apple. All the chewing calms me and the roughage fills me up just enough to satisfy me. Another good late night snack is *unbuttered* popcorn—one cup has only 23 calories!

I'm always amazed at how willpower seems to peter out late at night. You can abstain from sweets during all three dining hall meals, but the minute your roommate comes in with a bag of chocolate chip cookies you feel as if you're going to die unless you have one. All I can say is do whatever you have to do not to indulge in late night sweets. Run in place, do sit-ups, sit on your hands—drink two glasses of water or go to sleep—but don't eat those cookies! When it's late at night, all that sugar has nowhere to go except to your thighs.

These Are a Few of My Favorite Things

There are lots of *high-energy, low-calorie* snacks and drinks that you can make easily and store, especially if your dorm has a communal kitchen.

Here are some of my favorite foods that you can mix, make, and store yourself.

MY GRANOLA MIX

To a basic granola cereal that has no sugar, mix in portions that suit your taste:

sunflower seeds
flax
oats
pumpkin seeds
wheat flakes
raisins

Shake the dry mixture together and store it in an airtight container—a coffee can will do. This high-energy cereal is the perfect breakfast or snack—I pour soy milk over mine—but it is loaded with calories, so don't overdo. It's also great dry.

BROOKE'S BREAKFAST DRINK

Combine in a blender:

½ banana
½ cup of blueberries or strawberries (or any seasonal berry)
½ cup of soy milk or skim milk
1 raw egg
3 ice cubes

Blend until frothy. This fruit/protein drink will keep you in high gear until lunchtime, maybe even longer, and has only 225 calories. I guarantee that you won't taste the raw egg. This drink is a real rib-sticker.

LAZY AFTERNOON COCKTAIL

Combine in a blender:

1–2 tablespoons of brewer's yeast
1 cup of tomato juice or your favorite vegetable juice

Blend until thoroughly mixed. This terrific "cocktail" gives you instant refueling, and is the perfect energizer to drink one-half hour before you work out or exercise.

LOW-CAL, HIGH-ENERGY PROTEIN SNACKS

These low-cal, high-energy, or protein snacks provide the perfect *quick* pick-me-up to help you refuel in-between classes.

- a scoop of low-cal cottage cheese
- 1 hard-boiled egg
- a cup of low-cal yogurt
- an unlimited quantity of celery or carrots
- 1 oz. Swiss cheese
- 3½ oz. water-packed tuna
- 1 tablespoon of peanut butter on a rice cake.

FOOD FACTS

Have you sworn table sugar out of your life and replaced it with lower calorie honey? Do you snack on Triscuits instead of a chocolate chip cookie, because you are dieting? Here are some interesting caloric facts about some of your favorite foods that just may surprise you!

- Potato Treat: 1 big baked potato only has 145 calories (plain). Top with low fat yogurt, *not sour cream,* to add minimal calories. You'll never know the difference. French fries, on the other hand, have about 14 calories each.
- Water-packed tuna has about 160 fewer calories per 3½ ounce portion than oil-packed tuna.
- Honey has 61 calories per tablespoon compared to sugar that has only 46 calories per tablespoon.
- One scoop of chocolate ice cream has no more calories than seven Triscuits.
- One-half cup of frozen yogurt has 135–150 calories. One-half cup of rich (16 percent fat) ice cream has 165 calories. (That's only between 15–30 calories more!)
- Thirty pistachio nuts have 90 calories, while thirty cashews have a whopping 350 calories!
- Regular chewing gum has only 9 calories per stick while sugarless gum has 8 calories per stick.

- ❧ A bagel with 1 ounce of cream cheese has 270 calories (I just thought you'd like to know).
- ❧ If you have to have something sweet, fresh fruit is a wonderful low-calorie treat. *But be aware of carbohydrates:* 3 apricots (55 calories, 14 carbohydrates), ½ cup blueberries (45 calories, 11 carbohydrates), ¼ cantaloupe (41 calories, 10 carbohydrates), 1 nectarine (88 calories, 23 carbohydrates), 1 medium orange (64 calories, 15 carbohydrates), ½ papaya (60 calories, 15 carbohydrates), 1 peach (38 calories, 10 carbohydrates), 1 pear (86 calories, 20 carbohydrates), ½ cup fresh pineapple (48 calories, 9 carbohydrates), ½ cup raspberries (35 calories, 8 carbohydrates).
- ❧ Beware of dried fruits—they're high in calories! For instance, ½ cup of raisins has 240 calories, ½ cup dried apricots has 169 calories, 10 dried prunes have 215 calories.
- ❧ One potato chip has 15 calories—who can eat just one?
- ❧ While low in calories, most diet sodas are high in chemicals and salt—both contribute to water retention, bloat!

Why I Don't Smoke Cigarettes or Take Drugs, and Drink Only in Moderation

Cigarettes—yuck! I think that smoking is disgusting in every way. This is one new habit you don't want to start, and if you already have it, kick it.

You start to smoke in high school because you think that it makes you look grown up. For some reason, you think that having a cigarette hanging out of your mouth looks "cool." Actually, the reverse is true. Self-destructive behavior is neither attactive nor intelligent. Maybe you start smoking because you want to belong, fit in with your friends. Peer pressure can be a terrible thing—especially when it forces you to do something you know is bad for your health. Remember, from the moment you take that first puff, your body suffers.

In case you don't know, here are some of the awful things that smoking does to you and your body: nicotine residue from cigarettes collects on your teeth and turns them brown; it causes bad breath and a hacking cough. Your hair smells and your clothes closet stinks. Smoking

FRANCESCO SCAVULLO

is directly linked to lung cancer, doubles your chance of having a heart attack, and increases the risk of miscarriage and stillbirth. Knowing all this, why would anyone want to smoke? One of my favorite expressions says it all: "Stop before you start."

Many people in college smoke because they say it calms the jitters. I'll admit that the pressure of studying, writing papers, and taking exams is nerve-racking, but there are better ways to cope than lighting up. I'd rather be overweight than smoke. Chew some gum, take a walk, an aerobics class—run, breathe, exercise—enjoy the fresh air in your clean, healthy lungs. You'll have much more energy and feel better about yourself if you don't smoke. You'll also waste less time.

Some students turn to drugs as a coping mechanism. I can honestly say that I've never tried them, nor do I have any desire to. I'm not the least bit curious about how they make you feel, or what it's like to be high. To me, the negative consequences of taking drugs far outweigh any momentary thrill that they might provide. Every moment of my life is too precious for me to waste by being spaced out. I like clear vision and being in control at all times. I also respect myself too much to be self-destructive. Smoking, drugs, and alcohol can disrupt natural body rhythms, scramble your thinking, and ultimately take a toll on your physical resilience.

I realize that college is the perfect testing ground for everything—but why fool around with something that could potentially ruin and run your life? If I'm at a party where drugs surface, I leave. I don't care who's taking drugs, they'll always be a big no in my life. Aside from the important fact that they're illegal, I've got better things to do with my leisure time than fry my brains.

I feel the same way about excessive drinking. I might drink a little wine or champagne socially, but never to the point of getting high. Being *aware* all the time is important to me—you miss so much when you're high or drunk. And what about the next day? The consequences of excessive drinking aren't worth the high time that you might have had. You wake up with a hangover, facing all the foolish things you did or said, and the day is ruined because you feel miserable. The time is lost and suddenly you're one step behind.

If you're at a party that becomes too wild, or you're with a group of friends who are getting reckless with alcohol or drugs, take five and evaluate the whole situation. Is this something you really want to take part in? Are you prepared for the consequences—anything from waking up hung over, or where you don't want to be, to ending up in jail, arrested for driving under the influence of alcohol or using drugs. Think it through before you act, and consider all possible outcomes. Imagine confronting your parents with a phone call from jail when you're supposed to be on your own.

One of the hardest aspects of growing up is learning about limits—to realize when you've gone too far and need to moderate. It's not always easy to discern that fine line between enjoying your freedom and being reckless. When you're on your own, you're removed from parental guidance. You have to make your own choices. It's up to you to take care of yourself and your body. Remember, it's the only one you're ever going to have.

DEMARCHELIER

Fitness

I LOVE EXERCISING and I try not to go a single day without it. Working out makes me feel and look great all over. When combined with proper nutrition and plenty of sleep, I know that I'm giving myself the best care possible.

Exercise is necessary and vital for maintaining good physical and mental health. Not only does it tone, tighten, and trim your body, exercise also keeps your mind in order as it clears away the mental clutter. When I'm feeling overwhelmed with academic and career pressures, an exercise break will refresh and renew me so that I'm prepared to tackle everything! There's no doubt about it—exercise is the best stress reliever available and provides us with a much needed healthy balance in our active lives.

I know that I need exercise now more than ever—all those long hours of sitting and studying don't do much for anyone's body. So, no matter how tired I am, I always make time for some form of exercise. It's the perfect study break, and it's definitely better for you than a donut and a cup of coffee. Regardless of how tired you are when you begin, after a workout you will be energized, not exhausted, with extra energy to get you through the evening.

When I began college, I had even less time than before, so work-

DEMARCHELIER

ing exercise into my daily schedule was tough to do. I found that the best solution is to be flexible and to have several different routines so that no matter how my day shapes up, I can always work in some shaping up of my own.

A big plus of college life is the numerous sports activities available to you. Most colleges and universities offer field hockey, basketball, volleyball, tennis, raquetball, gymnastics, and swimming to name just a few—there really is something for everybody! When you get involved with a team, getting exercise is guaranteed because you must practice and work out with the team several times a week. As an added bonus you'll have lots of opportunities to make new friends and travel, as you visit other schools for games and matches.

If team participation isn't for you, look into the different areobic, calisthenic, and dance programs that your college physical education department offers. What about a course in jazz or tap dancing? Or maybe karate? You'll end up with a tight, toned, disciplined body as well as valuable self-defense skills.

No matter what program I choose, I try to do at least thirty minutes of some form of aerobic exercise (biking, aerobic dancing, fast walking) three times a week. The idea is to keep moving to sustain your increased heart rate. When you increase your heart rate for a period of time, you give your cardiovascular system (heart and lungs) a good workout and rev up your metabolism, burning off excess calories. Your metabolism continues to function at a higher rate for twenty-four hours after your aerobic workout, which means that you continue to burn calories more efficiently. After an aerobic workout, there's a feeling of healthy exhilaration as well as the satisfaction that you've done something good for yourself.

I've worked out and taken numerous classes at gyms and spas all over the world. But there are times when it's impossible for me to get to a class. So whether I'm in my dorm room or staying at a hotel, I'll put on the music for half an hour and just jog and jump around while keeping my arms moving. Or maybe I'll do a modified aerobic dance routine and a spot workout, using some of my favorite moves from the different classes I've taken. Here's a complete routine consisting of stretches, an aerobic dance routine, and a spot workout that I do on my own when I can't get to class.

If you have any medical problems check with your doctor before you try this routine or begin any exercise program. The following tips will also be helpful:

- ❧ Breathe regularly and evenly while you exercise.
- ❧ To provide extra cushioning and to prevent leg cramps, wear tennis or aerobic shoes while doing the aerobic dance routine.

All exercise photographs by Demarchelier.

LET'S STRETCH

Before you begin any form of exercise you should stretch out your body. Beginning with a series of stretches warms the muscles, prepares the body for a more vigorous workout, and helps prevent injury. The following series of stretches can be done alone, *anytime,* when you feel the need to loosen up and unkink those tension knots. They should *always* be done before the aerobics dance routine and the spot workout that follows.

YOU WILL FIND THAT ONE STRETCH FLOWS EASILY INTO THE NEXT.

Neck Rolls

POSITION: Stand with feet hip width apart, shoulders down, tummy tucked in and bottom tucked under.

SLOWLY
1. Touch right ear to right shoulder, slowly stretch back.
2. Drop head back, chin up. Slowly stretch forward.
3. Touch left ear to left shoulder, slowly stretch back.
4. Drop head forward, chin to chest, and slowly return to starting position.
5. Repeat in opposite direction.

Overhead Stretch

POSITION: Stand with feet hip width apart, hands overhead.

REALLY STRETCH

1. Reach overhead with your right hand, shifting your weight to your left hip and leg.
2. Reach overhead with your left hand, shifting your weight to your right hip and leg.
3. Alternate from side to side. Do 2 sets of 8 counts.

Side Stretches

POSITION: Stand with feet hip width apart.

AS YOU STRETCH PULL OUT OF YOURSELF—THINK "LONG"

1. Place left hand on hip and right hand overhead.
2. Stretch out and over your left foot.
3. Change arm position and repeat on opposite side.
4. Alternate from side to side. Do 2 sets of 8 counts.
5. In same position with right hand overhead, stretch to the left side.
6. Change arm position and repeat on opposite side.
7. Alternate from side to side. Do 2 sets of 8 counts.
8. Raise right elbow with left arm down. Stretch to the left.
9. Change arm position and repeat on opposite side.
10. Alternate from side to side. Do 2 sets of 8 counts.

Windmill Squat-Lunge Stretch

POSITION: Stand with feet a little wider than hip width apart.

1. Bend at the waist and flatten out your back. Hold for a count of 8.
2. Keep legs straight, bend at the waist and touch hands to the floor. Hold for a count of 8.
3. Stretch your left hand out behind you, and bring your right hand to your left foot. Touch your right ear to your left knee.
4. Repeat on opposite side.
5. Alternate from side to side. Do 2 sets of 8 counts.
6. Return to center position. Keep legs straight and touch hands to the floor. Hold for a count of 8.
7. Squat.

8. Stretch left leg out to the side. Shift your weight and lunge to the right.
9. Shift weight back towards center position and bring left leg in.
10. Stretch right leg out, shift your weight and lunge to the left.
11. Alternate from side to side. Do 1 set of 8 counts.
12. Return to center squat position.
13. Bring legs together and walk hands to center.
14. In this position, keep left foot flat on floor as you go up on right toe.
15. Repeat on opposite side.
16. Alternate from side to side. Do 2 sets of 8 counts.
17. Place feet and palms flat on the floor. Hold for a count of 8.

The Needle

POSITION: Feet and palms flat on floor (last position of Windmill-Squat Lunge).

1. Place your hands on your heels.
2. Slowly bring your head against your legs—or as close as you can. (The more you do this stretch, the easier it gets. Don't give up!)
3. Breathe deeply and hold for a count of 8.
4. Slowly unfold and come up: First the head, then the arms, now the spine, and finally the neck. As you work your way up shift your weight from left leg to right leg. Continue doing this until you are standing erect.

AEROBICS

Put on some rock and roll, or any lively music. Ideally, you should keep moving for a half-hour—but start slowly. When you're comfortable with a two minute period push yourself to do five minutes, then eight minutes, ten minutes . . . As your body gets stronger you will eventually reach a full thirty minutes. As you increase your time you can increase the counts in each move and the number of repetitions of the ·entire sequence.

Remember: Breathe deeply through the nose and out from the mouth. As your foot hits the ground, it should be *toe-heel* to avoid injury. Also, as you go from one move to the next *don't stop moving*.

Jogging

Begin with a light jog, moving your arms up and down.
1. Jog in place for 2 counts of 8.
2. Job backwards for 4 counts.
3. Jog forward for 4 counts.
4. Repeat 2 and 3.
5. Jog in circles for 2 sets of 8 counts.

Side Kicks

6. Kick right leg to the side—drop right arm and raise left elbow.
7. Kick left leg to the side—drop left arm, raise right elbow.
8. Alternate side kicks for 4 sets of 8 counts.

Jumps

9. Bounce low to the ground for 8 counts.
10. Jump high—knees to the right.
11. Jump high—knees to the left.
12. Repeat 9, 10, 11.
13. Bounce low to the ground 8 counts.

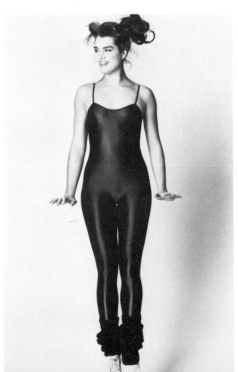 

Front Kicks

14. Bring your left knee across to your right elbow.
15. Bring your right knee across to your left elbow.
16. Alternate for 4 sets of 8 counts.
17. Finish the sequence with alternate show-girl kicks. Always keep your back straight—start with a lower kick if necessary.
18. Go back to JOGGING and repeat the entire sequence.

SPOT WORKOUT

The main problem with many exercise routines is that the movements are so big that individual muscles aren't worked. As you do this spot workout use small, tight, deep, slow, concentrated movements—as though you are working through the muscle and down to the bone. It helps if you imagine that there's some sort of resistance working against you at all times. This spot workout is guaranteed to tone, trim, and give muscle definition.

Arms

PULL THE LOAD
1. With knees slightly bent, bend elbows and curl fists up to underarms.
2. Keeping your fists tightly clenched, slowly pull your arms back behind you.
3. Slowly bend elbows and curl fists up to underarms. (The idea is to create resistance—imagine that you're pulling a heavy load up a hill that keeps sliding backwards.)
4. Do for 8 counts.

ARM CURLS

POSITION: Stand with feet hip width apart, knees slightly bent, arms outstretched, palms up.

1. Make fists.
2. Slowly bend your elbows and curl your fists up to shoulders. (Imagine some form of resistance.)
3. Fists still clenched, slowly stretch arms out to original position.
4. Repeat 1, 2, and 3 for 8 counts.
5. Curl and straighten left arm only for 8 counts.
6. Curl and straighten right arm only for 8 counts.

Waist

LONG STRETCH

POSITION: Stand, feet hip width apart.

1. With right arm extended straight toward the floor and the left arm extended toward the ceiling, bend sideways to the right.
2. Your right hand should cross your left thigh.
3. Repeat for opposite side.
4. Alternate from side to side. Do 2 sets of 8 counts.

HAND OVER HAND

POSITION: Lie flat with knees bent.

1. Pretend that you're pulling yourself up a pole, as you reach toward the ceiling hand over hand. Shoulders should come off the floor while torso remains stationary.
2. Do 4 sets of 8 counts, each time reaching high.

KNEE TOUCHES

POSITION: Lie flat with knees bent.

1. With hands on thighs, slide the hands down the thighs to the top of knees. Your upper body should curl off the floor.
2. Repeat 2 sets of 8 counts.

ELBOW-KNEE TWIST

POSITION: Lie flat with knees bent, hands clasped behind head.

1. Lift up and twist, touching right elbow to your left knee as you extend your right leg.
2. Bicycle by alternating and bringing your knees to opposite elbows.
3. Do 4 sets of 8 counts.

UPSIDE DOWN TOE-TOUCHES

POSITION: Lie flat with legs up and hands extended overhead.

1. Slowly reach up and touch your toes.
2. Do 2 sets of 8 counts.
3. Clasp your hands behind your head.
4. Pull your elbows together and pull yourself up until your elbows touch your knees.
5. Do 2 sets of 8 counts.

Hips, Thighs, and Buttocks

VARIATIONS ON THE LEG LIFT:

POSITION: Lie on your side supported by your right forearm, with your right leg extended and slightly bent. Your hips and knees should be aligned.

1. Raise and lower your left leg 8 counts with foot flexed, 8 times with toes pointed, and 8 counts with foot flexed.
2. With both knees bent and calves extended behind the body, raise and lower the left leg in small, tight movements. Make sure the hip and knee are in one horizontal line. Do 3 sets of 8 counts.
3. Now straighten your right leg and extend your left leg to the front of your body. Lift 8 counts flexed, 8 counts toes pointed, 8 counts foot flexed.
4. Bend left knee and place left foot on the floor close to body. Raise and lower the right leg. Do 3 sets of 8 counts.
5. Repeat entire sequence on opposite side.

PELVIS TILT

POSITION: Lie flat with knees bent, feet flat on floor, hands resting on stomach.

1. Lift the pelvis off the floor and tighten buttock muscles while keeping upper back on floor.
2. Do 8 lifts. (This should be small and tight.)
3. Lift pelvis and hold for 8 counts.
4. Repeat with knees touching and feet hip width apart and flat on the floor.

FLUTTER KICK

POSITION: On hands and knees, weight equally distributed.

1. Raise your right leg behind you, keeping thigh and hip aligned and foot flexed.
2. Bring heel toward buttock.
3. Kick out so thigh and calf make 45 degree angle.
4. Do 2 sets of 8 counts.
5. Repeat for opposite side.

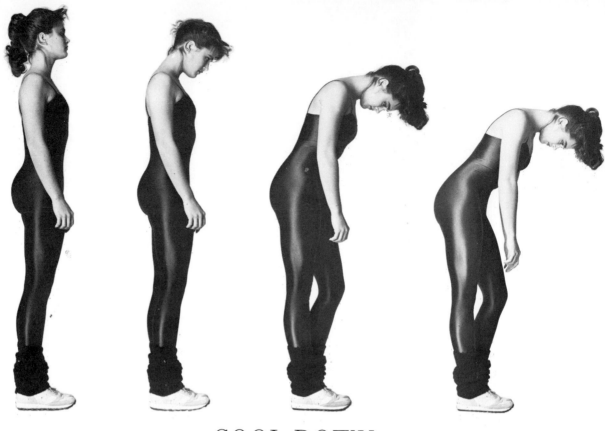

COOL DOWN

Finish your aerobic dance routine and spot workout with some simple cool down stretches. Use this time for deep breathing and to relax your mind and body. The cool down helps your muscles ease into their normal workload.

First, repeat The Needle—only this time reverse it.

1. Begin standing erect.
2. Slowly fold over and go down: first the neck, than the spine, than the arms and finally the head—bringing it against your legs.
3. As you work your way down, shift your weight from your left leg to your right leg. Continue doing this until you are folded over.

4. Hold the position and breathe deeply for 8 *slow* counts. NOW SQUAT AND SIT ON THE FLOOR.
5. Stretch your legs out in front of you.
6. Reach your arms up overhead, really stretching out of your body, and stretch over to your feet.
7. As you deep-breathe, ease into the final position: feet flexed, hands around heels and elbows to the floor. Work with your breath, easing into the stretch.
8. Ahhhhhhhh . . . .

DEMARCHELIER

Looks

I DO BELIEVE that what's inside is important—that your looks just take you so far—*but looks do count.* Why else is there so much emphasis placed on fitness, health, and beauty? First impressions and initial attractions are based on your appearance. And when you feel that you look good you're happier and much more outgoing.

As you start college and become immersed in many different and new activities, time becomes scarce. Often your appearance and personal hygiene are the first things that get neglected as you meet the challenges of this new life-style. But no matter how little time you have, it's extremely important that you continue to pamper your skin and hair, get enough sleep, and start each day in fresh, clean clothes. Fancy outfits and elaborate makeup and hairstyles are not necessary, but you always want to look clean and fresh—even if it means starting your day one-half hour earlier. Believe me, you'll feel much better about yourself if you do.

Looking good gives me the confidence to approach new challenges and people—it frees me from distracting worries (Have I gained weight? Are my clothes wrong?) and lets me focus on other aspects of my life. Let's face it, *your looks are your starting point,* so it's worth a little thought and effort to start each day feeling positive about what you see in the mirror before you sail out the door! I hope people never stop saying that I'm beautiful—and I'm willing to earn that compliment. Nothing comes easy.

DEMARCHELIER

SKIN CARE

For me, good looks depend—first and foremost—on my skin. The secret to having great looking skin is cleanliness. I know that when my skin is clean and clear I radiate. You can never be too young to start pampering your skin. Even if you have a peaches-and-cream complexion, you should be moisturizing now. It's when you take your skin for granted that you get into trouble.

My best tip for having great-looking skin, regardless of your skin type, is never to go to sleep with your makeup on. If you do, it will settle in your pores and prevent your skin from "breathing," which can lead to pimples and blackheads. Even though you go to bed with every smidgen of makeup removed, you should start each day with a *clean sweep,* getting rid of the oils and perspiration that accumulate overnight.

My Routine

I consider myself lucky to have normal skin. As long as I follow my cleansing routine, I have few skin problems or breakouts. My nighttime cleansing-beauty ritual is good for anyone with *normal* skin.

1. First I work on my eyes with eye makeup remover pads. (Any drugstore carries them, or you can use a nonoily liquid cleanser on a cotton ball.)
2. Next I go over my entire face with a heavy cream cleanser—this is especially important if I've been modeling or acting, and I've been heavily made-up. I really work the cream into my skin in an upward motion. Why give gravity any help?
3. I wipe off the heavy cream cleanser with cotton pads (tissues are too harsh on anyone's skin) and then wash my face with glycerine soap and water. My dermatologist started me on glycerine soap when I was nine years old.

DEMARCHELIER

DEMARCHELIER

DEMARCHELIER

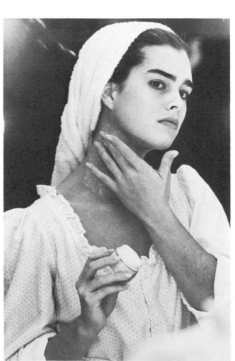

DEMARCHELIER

4. I finish with a light astringent or freshener to close my pores and tone my skin. Now my skin is really clean and ready to be moisturized for the night.

5. I put vitamin E oil around my eyes—careful not to get any in my eye—especially where "laugh lines" are apt to appear. The final touch is a night cream—and, of course, I remember to work some into my neck too! P.S. This entire routine should always include the neck.

Since I clean my face so well at night, I usually begin my day with a splash of water without soap, or just a freshener—and a light moisturizer. Whether or not I decide to wear makeup, my face is prepared for the day.

$$H_2O + ASTRINGENT + MOISTURIZER =$$

RISKO

Oily Skin

If your skin is oily, you are probably more prone to breakouts. This can be maddening. Ever notice how the breakout inevitably occurs right before something important comes up? But more about breakouts later.

When it comes to cleansing oily skin you're better off avoiding cream cleansers, and using a good natural soap for oily skin and a strong astringent instead. Just because your skin is oily, don't skip the moisturizer—even acne-prone skin needs added moisture to keep it smooth and soft. Check out the many light, oil-free moisturizers that are made for oily complexions.

A common mistake that people with oily skin make is overwashing. Too much rubbing and scrubbing can irritate sensitive skin follicles, causing inflammation. Overstimulating your skin will also cause your glands to produce even more oil—the last thing you need! Limit your use of grainy cleaners and buff-puffs to a couple of times a week; other times a strong nubby washcloth will do.

One of the best tools for combating oily skin is a creamy clay-based mask. A good clay mask will draw impurities from the pores, lift away dead surface skin, absorb excess oil, and stimulate your circulation—leaving you with a healthy glow. There are all kinds of clay masks available in drugstores and health-food stores, or you can easily make your own using *fuller's earth* (also available at drugstores).

To make your own *herbal clay mask* combine 1 tablespoon of fuller's earth, 1 tablespoon of rubbing alcohol, and 1 tablespoon of hot sage or chamomile tea (both teas have healing qualities). Mix these three ingredients to a paste consistency, adding more tea if necessary. After applying to your face let the mask dry for 15–25 minutes. Use this time to relax with your favorite magazine. You'll feel a tightening sensation. Wash off with warm water, then cool water. Finish with an appropriate astringent and moisturizer.

Another good oil-absorbing, deep pore cleanser is a *brewer's yeast and honey mask*. Brewer's yeast draws and cleanses while the honey heals and disinfects. To 1 tablespoon of brewer's yeast add enough honey to make a paste. Apply and remove as above. Finish with your astringent and moisturizer.

Dry Skin

If your skin is dry you'll want to use cleansing creams, alcohol-free astringents or toners, and heavy moisturizers. Facial soap and water should be used sparingly—look for hypoallergenic and natural cream soaps. For you, it is best to avoid all deodorant soaps or soaps with artificial coloring and chemicals. Wash your skin gently, using only your hands.

Of course your cleansing routine will be determined by just how dry your skin actually is. In extreme cases, when there is flaking and itching you should see a dermatologist. To play it safe, stick with hypoallergenic products and when you're making up, try oil-based foundations with extra emollients, and cream blushers.

Dry skin should be treated to a mask too, but avoid grainy, harsh, scrubbing masks—they'll only irritate and make your skin dryer. Try a deep cleansing, moisturizing mask prepared especially for dry skin. Or give yourself a terrific facial with two eggs. The lecithin in egg yolk smoothes the skin.

Beat two raw eggs together and apply to your clean face with cotton balls. When your face feels stiff and the egg has hardened, rinse well with warm water. If you want to be even more natural, wipe your face with cucumber slices instead of your usual toner. Then moisturize.

Combination Skin

Combination skin means that you're prone to oiliness on the forehead, nose, and chin (this is known as the T-zone) and dryness on your cheeks. Probably the most important cleansing secret to remember when you

RISKO

have combination skin is to treat each area individually. This may seem like extra work, but it's well worth the time and effort. For combination skin use a facial soap and water and an alcohol based astringent on your forehead, nose and chin. A cleansing cream and an alcohol-free astringent will be milder for your cheeks.

When it comes to using masks on combination skin I think you'll want to alternate. Try using a clay-based mask one week and a deep moisturizing mask the next week. Again you'll have to experiment until you find the right combination for your combination skin.

If you have access to a stove or hot plate, a wonderful cleansing pick-me-up for combination and normal skin is a peppermint steam. All you have to do is toss a handful of peppermint leaves into a pot of boiling water (let them steep for a few minutes), then drape a towel over your head, and lean over the pot for 3–4 minutes. Make sure that you turn off the heat before you steam yourself.

Breakout Blues

You've cleansed and pampered your skin to the hilt. But suddenly—*zap!*—there's a pimple or two invading your face. First and foremost, *don't pick!* I know it's tempting, but don't, because you will only irritate your skin. The best thing you can do is clean your face thoroughly, dab on a little medicated cover-up and leave pimples alone. They will eventually dry out. Try not to wear any foundation or blusher for a day or two so that your skin can breathe and heal naturally.

If you're having a full-fledged breakout, avoid grainy cleansers and scrubbing masks. Their abrasive action will open up the pimples, cause them to spread, and keep them from healing properly. Also be aware of the cosmetics you're using. If it seems that your breakouts coincide with a certain blusher or foundation you wear, throw it out!

Frequent breakouts or severe acne need a dermatologist's attention. There are lots of new topical and oral medications available, and I hear from my friends that they can really help.

Some Tried and True Skin Care Do's and Don'ts

❧ Don't cheat on your cleansing program, only to have to compensate with medicated cover-ups.

❧ Don't keep your makeup *forever*. Toss out what's left and restock *every three months* (especially mascara, cream blushers, and foundations—bacteria breeds in moisture).

❧ When applying eye oils and eye creams always lightly pat them around your eyes with your index finger.

❧ Don't forget your ears! I'm always using Q-tips—just don't stick them too far into your ear canal.

❧ Don't ever use a friend's makeup or acne medication—you may get more than you bargained for.

❧ Do rinse your face at least fifteen times with tepid water to remove every trace of soap.

❧ Don't constantly put your hands to your face. The bacteria from your hands can get in your pores and provoke breakouts.

❧ Do treat your skin gently. Excessive rubbing and general manhandling isn't good for anyone's skin.

❧ Bangs or any hair hanging onto your face can promote blemishes.

DEMARCHELIER

SLEEP

Next to cleanliness, the best thing you can do for your complexion is *sleep!* Getting enough rest is one of the best beauty treatments readily available to you. I know the minute I don't get enough sleep I can see the difference—my skin breaks out and dark circles appear under my eyes.

Unfortunately, it's hard to make time for sleep when you're at college or just starting out on your own. It takes discipline to say goodnight to your friends and get those forty winks, especially when you'd rather stay up all night talking and socializing. And what about those sleepless nights because of too much coffee and exam anxiety? There's nothing worse than lying in bed wide awake, when you know that you should be asleep. Whether it's studying and classes, or working, plus a social life—no one wants to give sleep top priority, but we should. I know my next day's performance definitely depends on how much sleep I've gotten.

Prelude To Sleep

Preparing for a good night's sleep is a quiet, pleasant time for me. The little routines and rituals I go through are a necessary part of unwinding so that when I slip between the sheets I just melt.

I've got to be clean when I go to sleep, because when I'm clean and my surroundings are tidy I'm able to relax. This means fresh sheets, clean nightgown—all my papers and books in order. I can't sleep when there's chaos around me.

Once I'm ready for bed I check my alarm and then snuggle under the covers. Usually I'm so tired that I barely make it through my prayers. If I do, and I feel restless, I start thinking of something happy, like riding

DEMARCHELIER

one of my horses or being with someone I like—or maybe I think about a movie set I've been on and what it was like. Sometimes I'll just make up wonderful stories that transport me into a deep sleep.

I avoid counting sheep because I get obsessed with the number of sheep jumping, and I try not to think about anything negative that will make me worry—worry is the sleep thief. If you start indulging in thoughts like, "What if *this* happens tomorrow," or "Did I do well on my test today?" or "What if he doesn't like me as much as I like him . . . ," you'll never get to sleep. When you are overwhelmed with worry, remind yourself that yesterday is gone and tomorrow isn't here yet—there is only *now,* which is the warm, wonderful bed where you are safe and secure.

To me, sleep is like a gift. If you've had a really rotten day, sleep is your chance to escape. When you're asleep you don't have to talk, you don't have to be *on,* and you don't have to do anything but be inside yourself. So indulge in sleep whenever you can, appreciate it, and enjoy it.

Sleep Tricks

Having a hard time drifting off? Here are a few of my favorite sleep tricks, and one or two that my friends swear by.

DEMARCHELIER

❧ If you have a lot on your mind before bedtime, and you're afraid you'll forget things that need to be done tomorrow, make a list and leave it beside your bed. If you work yourself into a panic, you can refer to this list and add to it. Knowing that everything you need to do tomorrow is on that list can relieve worry and give you peace of mind. You might want to keep a flashlight and pen beside your bed, too. Turning the lights off and on can disturb a roommate.

❧ I don't like milk, but I've been told that a warm mug of milk with a tablespoon of honey does wonders to soothe and unravel any raw edges left over from a hectic day.

❧ I love to sip a hot cup of chamomile tea while I get ready for bed—many believe that it's a light, natural sedative.

DEMARCHELIER

❧ Avoid spicy foods or late night pizza, unless you want your stomach to keep you awake. If you must indulge before bed try a dish of low-fat ice cream—it's kind to your waistline and the calcium in ice cream is good for your nerves.

❧ Absolute dark a must? Invest in a sleep mask.

❧ Splurge on your favorite bedding. Satin sheets, cotton sheets, linen sheets, flannel sheets—whatever feels best to you. And what about an electric blanket? There's nothing more relaxing than crawling into a warm, cozy bed on a cold winter's night.

❧ If your body feels tense, slip into a nice hot steamy bath—close your eyes and fantasize . . .

❧ If you still feel tense after a hot bath try this all-over body de-tenser. (Believe it or not, by purposely tensing your body you can relax it.) Begin with your toes and tense. Hold for a count of ten. Release. Now tense your whole foot. Hold for a count of ten. Release. Now tense your foot and calf. Hold for a count of ten. Release. Now tense your foot, calf, and thigh. Hold for a count of ten. Release. Repeat with the opposite leg; tense arms, neck, and face. Finish by tensing your whole body simultaneously for a count of ten. Release. If you're still awake, you should be very relaxed. Remember to do this very slowly and in a relaxed fashion—don't hurry through it.

❧ Try soothing music: harp music, soft piano, flute, or maybe environment music. There are lots of tapes and records available geared for relaxing and sleep.

❧ If you've tried all these tricks and you're still wide awake (we all have those nights once in a while) don't drive yourself crazy. Get up and make the most of your time. Read a book, work on a paper, do something you really enjoy, something you don't have the time for during your busy schedule. But don't lie there fretting because you can't sleep. I have one friend who has two or three sleepless nights a month. So she gets up and works on her stamp collection. (And she only works on it when she can't sleep—this makes it special.) Usually after she's into it for an hour she's yawning and ready for bed.

⋑ If you share your room with a roommate, you may want to work out some "sleep agreements": An agreed time for lights out, stereo off, and a last call for visitors and friends.

⋑ A set of headphones can help you escape by blocking out dorm noise without disturbing your roommate.

⋑ Keep a set of ear plugs available for when late night dorm activities get out of hand.

The 20 Minute Catnap Refresher

When you've had a hectic day and you know you're going to have an even crazier night, take a 20 minute catnap refresher in the afternoon. This followed by ten minutes of "lazy afternoon" exercises (see my fitness section) will energize you for the evening.

The best thing to do is to lie down and place a cool, wet cloth over your eyes to refresh them. Now just relax—you'll probably drift into that peaceful state between deep sleep and consciousness, which is similar to meditating. Try to limit your nap to 20 minutes, otherwise you may go into a very deep sleep and risk waking feeling groggy and disoriented instead of refreshed.

As hard as it might be in a dorm, establish good sleep habits. We can get by with a minimal amount of sleep for a while, but eventually it will catch up with us. Dark circles, low energy, irritability—who needs it. Getting a good night's sleep should be as automatic as brushing your teeth.

MAKEUP

Rather than being artificial, your makeup will be artful if you know what you're doing. When it comes to applying makeup, I've had some of the best teachers. The most famous makeup artists in the world have worked on my face. Each time I learn a new trick or look, I go home and practice it in front of the mirror until I've gotten it just right. As a result, I've got loads of tricks and tips up my sleeve for any occasion—whether it's a guest appearance at the Academy Awards or a night out on the town with my friends.

On a day-by-day basis, and especially while I'm busy with my studies at Princeton, I think clean and natural is best. But clean and natural does not mean no makeup. I don't feel dressed unless I'm wearing blusher, lip gloss and mascara. Although I do go bare-faced around the house—just tons of moisturizer! I consider these *the basics* that are necessary to bring a little life to your face—especially important when your day starts at 7 A.M. Don't we all need a little color, a little shine, and an eye-opener? Here are some of my best tips for applying *the basics,* as well as some super *eye-openers* and *lip-tricks.*

Mascara

When I put on makeup I always do my eyes first—even if it's just mascara. You can use cream mascara that comes in a tube with a wand or use a cake type that comes with a brush and must be mixed with water. I prefer cream mascara because it's easier to use. Basically, there are three types of cream mascaras to choose from:

WATERPROOF—This type is my favorite because it lasts and lasts without smudging or flaking. You can swim with it on, shower with it on, and still have great, long-looking lashes.

LASH BUILDING—This mascara thickens and lengthens your lashes with artificial lashlike fibers. You're probably better off staying away from this type if you wear contact lenses because the fibers can shed or flake off, get in your eyes and under your lens.

NATURAL—This mascara subtly defines and colors. It's a good mascara to use when you want just a hint of color. It usually washes off with soap and water, or cleanses off very easily.

Before you apply the mascara of your choice you might want to curl your lashes—this will open your eyes up even more. Just make sure

DEMARCHELIER

DEMARCHELIER

that you always curl your lashes before applying mascara. If you do it afterwards, you might break off some of your lashes. Also, when curling your lashes, open up the eyelash curler completely before you pull it away from your eye. Otherwise you could pull out some of your lashes—ouch!

The best way to apply mascara is in 3–4 very thin layers, allowing each layer to dry between applications. After each layer dries separate your lashes with an eyebrow brush. Some mascaras come with a comb applicator, perfect for separating lashes. And remember to apply mascara to both your top and bottom lashes for balance.

If your lashes are really thin, try dusting them with a little translucent powder before you begin applying the layers of mascara. This will make your lashes look thicker. Be careful of contact lenses here too!

A final word on mascara and general eyelash care: *Always* remove your mascara before going to sleep and treat your lashes to a conditioning coat of petroleum jelly at least three times a week.

Eye-openers

Now for some of my favorite *eye-openers*—eye "looks" guaranteed to perk up tired eyes (after all those long hours of studying) and to turn your schoolgirl eyes into sexy, sultry knockouts!

❧ To get the best results hold a mirror under your chin and look down when applying mascara to your upper lashes. Undoubtedly, you will have better control.

❧ For tired, bloodshot eyes, I recommend using eyedrops. One of my favorite camouflage tricks is to rim the inside of my lower lashes with a blue pencil and use dark blue mascara on my lashes. This whitens and brightens no matter what color your eyes are.

❧ I picked up the best trick to conteract puffy eyes (while on the set of *Wet Gold,* a television movie I made): Chill two spoons in ice water and hold them—bowl side in—against your eyes. The cold will reduce redness and swelling in a few minutes.

❧ To create an outrageous look that's perfect for the disco, I outline my top and bottom lashes with a thin line of green shadow and finish with *red* mascara.

❧ Smudge a little pale blue frosted eye shadow underneath your lower lids—it will attract the light and enhance your eyes.

❧ Smudge a dot of blue liner on the center of your upper lids—this will draw attention upwards so that your eyes look bigger and more open.

RISKO

- For a sexy, smouldering nighttime look: Line the upper lid as close to the lashline as possible with a frosted liner. Line the lower lashes with a matte liner in a complementary color. Smudge lines with your fingertip or a sponge-ended eye pencil.
- Soft-textured pencils are easiest to work with and provide richer color.
- Avoid eye pencil breakage—store your eye pencils in the refrigerator until you're ready to use them.
- Experiment with the new colored mascaras—they're great for creating fresh-looking eyes and they give the eyes a sexy softness. They come in wonderful greens, reds, violets, blues, and burgundies.
- For "eye appeal" if you wear glasses: First remember that strong makeup colors might compete or clash with frames. Soft colors will give your eyes a sexy look. *Farsighted* lenses will magnify your eyes. You can play down their size by brushing a taupe or pale grey shadow along the crease. Blend up to the outer corner of the brow. Also remove any excess mascara with a lash comb or spiral brush—little clumps left behind will also be magnified and perhaps fall into the eye. *Nearsighted* lenses will make your eyes appear smaller, so open them up by using pink highlighter on the brow bone and a neutral color along the lid. Intensify the color just above the lashes and fade out towards the outer corner. Softly underline the lower lashes with eyeliner.

Blusher

Before I apply any blusher or makeup I wake up my skin and tighten my pores with ice water. Simply wrap a few ice cubes in a face cloth and run it all over your face and neck—it feels terrific! Pat dry and apply your moisturizer (great to do while you skin is still cool) and always allow it to dry completely before you apply your blusher.

I like to use a powder blusher. It's easy to blend so that it always looks natural and it works well on all skin types. Use a dry, clean, fluffy

DEMARCHELIER

brush to soften the color and to blend the edges. If you have excessively dry skin you might want to use a cream blusher—just make sure that you blend it well.

One of the most common makeup mistakes is applying blusher to the wrong places. Since blusher should highlight your bone structure and balance your face, it is applied according to your facial shape. Here are some tips for the various facial shapes:

OVAL—You have what is considered the ideal face. Your forehead is wider than your chin, your cheekbones are dominant, and your face tapers to a narrow chin. To apply blusher: With your fingertips find the most prominent part of your cheekbones. Start your blusher at this spot and blend it up towards your temples.

TRIANGULAR—Your wide forehead and high cheekbones taper to a narrow chin. To apply blusher: Blusher should be applied in a sideways V on the cheekbones and blended up to the temples. Extend blusher over the eyebrows towards, but not to, the center of the forehead. This will balance your forehead with the rest of your face. Do not apply blusher on your chin.

RECTANGULAR—Your face is an elongated square shape with your forehead about the same width as your cheekbones and jaw. To apply blusher: Begin blusher on the outer edges of your cheekbones below the outer corner of your eyes. Blending up to the temples will give more width to your face. Do not blend blusher lower than the tip of your nose.

SQUARE—Your squared forehead is about the same width as your cheekbones and jaws, with a squared jaw being dominant. To apply blusher: Begin blusher on the cheekbones; your starting point is the center of each eye. Blend blusher up towards the temples. You can soften the square angle of your face if you apply a dot of blusher on the center of your forehead and chin.

ROUND—Your face is just about as wide as it is long and the widest part is at the cheeks. To apply blusher: You can slenderize your face by applying blusher in a sideways V on cheekbones. Blend up towards your temples. A touch of blusher on your chin will give the illusion of a longer face.

RISKO

You can create the illusion of high cheekbones by using a lighter and darker tone of the same color. Apply the deeper shade in the hollow areas under your cheekbones and the lighter shade *directly* above it. Carefully blend the two for an even-toned look.

Finding the right blusher color is something you're going to have to experiment with. Try to avoid colors that overwhelm and contrast too sharply with your natural skin tone. For instance, a bright red blusher will look too harsh on fair skin; pale pink will look faded on olive skin. No matter how well you blend, the wrong color of blusher still won't look natural. Also remember that smaller faces look best with a brighter blusher while fuller, larger faces require more subtle tones.

When working with eye and lip colors, color-key your blusher for a harmonizing effect. For instance, if you're using peaches, rusts, and browns on your eyes and lips you'll want to use a peach-colored blusher. Lavenders, pinks, purples, and greys should be coordinated with pink, rose, or plum-colored blusher.

A Word about Foundation

If you don't need foundation, don't wear it. Unless I'm doing a photo session, when I need a matte finish, I try to stick with blusher and a light brushing of translucent powder. To me, a little clean shine is healthy-looking. People who wear tons of foundation look almost dead with such a heavy matte finish—not to mention what it does to your skin! It also enhances wrinkles and laugh lines. But if you think you really need it or just want to wear it because you don't feel dressed without it, here are some foundation fundamentals to consider.

COLOR—The color of foundation you choose should match your skin tone as closely as possible. In a natural light, test several tints on your jawline. You'll want to choose the foundation that looks "nearly invisible" on your skin but gives a clear, finished appearance.

FINISH—Different types of foundations will provide you with varying degrees of coverage, from sheer to maximum, and different fin-

ishes, from dewy to matte. You'll also want to consider your skin type when choosing a foundation. Oily skin needs a water-based foundation with shine-stopping ingredients like talc. Dry skins will benefit from an emollient-rich foundation.

APPLICATION TIPS

- ⇝ Always test foundation before buying—the color printed on the label might not be accurate. Test it on your jawline, not your wrist or hand where skin color and texure is different.
- ⇝ When in doubt, a lighter shade of foundation is safer than the darker shade.
- ⇝ For concealing dark circles, use a foundation one shade lighter than your all-over foundation.
- ⇝ Don't forget your earlobes and neckline when applying foundation.
- ⇝ For a "seamless finish" run moistened fingers into your hairline and below chinline down to the neck area after foundation has been applied.

❧ After applying foundation blot gently with a tissue to remove any excess. This is the secret for the most *natural look*.

❧ For a dewy finish set foundation with an all-over "whoosh" of mineral water, but ever so misty.

❧ For a matte finish try a light dusting of translucent powder avoiding the eye area.

Lips

When you pamper your face with good cleansing habits, moisturizers and masks, don't forget your lips—they need special care too! You'll keep them kissing-soft by brushing them with a soft toothbrush and a little lip balm or petroleum jelly once or twice a week. Doing this removes any chapped, peeling skin, and deep-moisturizes. This stimulation will flush their color, too. Finish with a coat of petroleum jelly—it's a great natural lip gloss. Keeping your lips glossed at all times will prevent you from licking your lips, which is specially drying in the sun or cold.

I always wear lip gloss, but sometimes I want something more. Maybe a little color, or maybe something provocative for a big night out. These are just a few of my favorite *lip-tricks*. Some are basic and one or two are just a little bit wild and crazy—and definitely fun!

❧ Lipstick will wear longer if you apply a light coat of foundation and/or face powder on your lips before applying lip liner and color.

❧ In your bag of tricks a lip brush is a must! It will give you an exacting application, can be used to vary the depth of color, and is perfect for blending.

❧ You can use eye pencils and eye colors on your mouth, but don't use lip colors on your eyes—they're too harsh for the delicate skin that surrounds your eyes.

❧ Use gold or pearlized colors to highlight your lips for a glamorous evening look.

❧ *To make full lips look thinner:* Line your lips with lip-liner just *inside* your natural lipline, defining the corners too. Wear soft, medium-to-dark cream colors. Stay away from bright colors, frosts, and glosses.

- *To make thin lips look fuller:* Line your lips with lip-liner around the *outer* edge of your natural lipline. Use light-to-medium colors, frosts, and glosses.

- If one of your lips is larger than the other, a lipstick brush can save the day. Balance the size difference by either emphasizing the thinner lip or diminishing the fuller, whichever suits your face better.

- When you want more than a lip gloss you can add subtle color with a lip-liner. First moisten your lips with a lip balm. Blot excess. Next, using a lip pencil in a soft red or pink, lightly outline your mouth. Take a lip brush and smudge the outline as you carefully work the color evenly into your lips.

- A matte pink shade with blue undertones will give your teeth a whiter, brighter look. Soft shades of peach, apricot, rust, and berry are also flattering. Scarlet lips may make your teeth look duller or even discolored.

- Using a lip brush, combine lip gloss and color together for a moist, translucent looking mouth.

- For a really full, pouty mouth use a matte lipstick. Then dot the center of your lower lip with a burst of fuschia lip color or gold powder. Wow!

- Have a suntan? Try outlining your lips with gold and fill them in with a bronze or brown shade. Finish with a clear gloss.

- Carefully blend your lip-liner for natural looking lips—you don't want your lips to look drawn on.

HAIR

Graduation from high school, entering college, or going out into the world for your first "real" job may inspire you to make a hair change. Maybe you've had hair way down to there, but you think that you'd like a more sophisticated look. Perhaps you'd like to turn your stick-straight hair into a head of massive curls. Whatever you decide, try to keep your new hairstyle as simple and carefree as possible. Getting a new haircut that demands a lot of complicated blow-drying, setting, etc., just isn't practical and is no longer necessary for a great look. The new cuts, mousses, and styling gels make hair care simpler than it's ever been. With just a puff of mousse you can add height, curls, or slicked back control to almost any hairstyle—now that's progress!

If you are thinking of a change—a new cut, perm, a little color, whatever—find the *right* hairdresser! Don't leave the fate of your locks in the hands of inventive friends or an anonymous hairdresser. I have one friend who wanted to perm her very long hair and save money at the same time. She went for the "$6 Special" at a local trade school where the students learn on your hair. She hadn't known anyone who had ever used this particular school and she didn't bother to investigate its reputation. Even worse, rather than giving the place a try with a simple procedure—like a trim—she jumped right in with a permanent, a tricky proposition in the best of places. What a disaster! For her $6 she ended up with at least $300 worth of trouble, not to mention what her hair looked like. Their perm solution was left on too long and her hair was burned. It broke off at the crown of her head and was a mass of frizz down her back. Her hair was such a mess that she couldn't get a comb through it. She finally ended up at a real salon for repair work where they cut her hair off and started her on an extensive conditioning program to bring her hair back to life.

Your best bet in finding a good haircutter is word of mouth. Of course, looks that you admire on others are a beauty salon's best advertisement. Visit the shop before your appointment and see how things are run. Beware of the salon that's all tinsel and glitter—it has nothing to do with the talent of the hairdressers. Is the salon clean and efficiently run? Are lots of people being taken care of or does it seem to be an *off* day? The busier the salon the better, but you don't want to be kept waiting for hours either.

If you're planning a drastic change, you might want to test the hairdresser first. Go in for a harmless shampoo, trim, blow-dry or set. How does the hairdresser handle your hair? Does he concentrate on what he's doing or does he chatter too much? Does he seem exacting? A new hairdresser should be focusing on your hair, since he's never worked with it before. He should also evaluate it dry, before he begins, so that he can get a good idea of how your hair lies against your head.

After the hairdresser has passed your initial test you're ready to make your change. Go through the fashion magazines and collect pictures of styles you like—but be realistic! Do you really want to turn your stick-straight hair into the Orphan Annie look? Or blow-dry your curly hair every day into a straight, blunt bob? Work with your hair's natural color and texture—not against it. Remember that any coloring or perming, no matter how expertly done, will change the condition and texture of your hair so that some of its natural vitality will be lost. Really think about what you want before you make the change. Your hairdresser will probably have some ideas about what will work best with facial shape, hair texture, and your weight.

If you're thinking of going with the current fad, remember that you won't be able to change it back magically if you don't like it. Consider a style that's easy to take care of, will work for all your moods, and one that you can live with for a long period of time. Whatever you do, *don't* (and I repeat don't) wait until the day of the prom or your sister's wedding to treat yourself to something new.

Some Basic Hair Care

Depending on your hair type—normal, dry, oily—find a system of shampooing and conditioning that works best for you. A good conditioner gives you body and shine while it makes your hair easy to comb.

Sometimes I'll put a heavy conditioner on my hair (like a deep, penetrating oil), braid my hair, and just leave it for 24 hours. This is

great to do during exam period because you don't have to think about your hair. After I wash the oil out, my hair has lots of shine and body. This type of deep conditioning works well in the summer to counteract the sun's drying effects.

You might also want to try this 30-minute at-home conditioner: Mix together one egg yolk and ¼ cup of castor oil and apply to your hair. Wrap your hair in plastic (household plastic wrap or a large plastic bag will work), rather than a towel. This will help the mixture penetrate deeply. After 30 minutes thoroughly rinse with warm water and shampoo lightly.

If your hair has gone limp, but you don't have the time to shampoo, try the baby powder trick. Lightly brush a baby powder that contains cornstarch through your hair. First bend your head over and brush your hair forward. Apply the powder to your brush and add more at regular intervals. Starting at the nape of your neck, brush your hair back into place as you gradually stand up. By brushing this way the powder will be distributed evenly. This technique will remove excess oil and add volume.

You'll want to keep your hair accessories (brushes, combs, barettes, headbands, etc.) clean—otherwise the dirt and oil buildup will end up back in your hair. Soaking your hair accessories once a week in warm sudsy water should do the trick. And you can remove hair buildup that accumulates in your brushes with a brush cleaner, available at any variety store.

When your hair is wet it stretches and is also very weak, so handle it with care. The following tips will prevent unnecessary tangling, splitting, and breaking:

- ⇒ Brush your hair free of any tangles before you shampoo. When you shampoo, work the lather into your scalp first, using your fingertips (not fingernails) to massage your scalp. Gently work the lather down from the roots to the ends of your hair.
- ⇒ Piling soapy hair on top of your head, while you're washing it, can create tangles.
- ⇒ Always *pat* and squeeze your hair dry. Avoid rubbing.
- ⇒ Always comb out your wet hair—never brush—you'll find combing from the ends first, then working your way up to the roots is a foolproof way of preventing any tangling.

Curling irons (wands) and hot rollers can damage your hair if they are used improperly. Before you use either one, treat your hair with a heat-styling product, which will prevent your hair from becoming dry and fly-away. Remember to wind your dry or slightly damp (never wet) hair carefully around curling irons and rollers. Also unwind carefully—pulling rollers out in a hurry can leave you with a tangled mess.

I've invested in a new type of hot roller with no prongs to pull the hair. A soft, natural-type curler, to which the hair clings, has replaced the prongs, which can be damaging to your hair. They're terrific—they reduce breakage and tangles.

Blow-drying Tips

Blow-drying can do wonders for all types of hair. It provides instant volume, making even baby-fine hair look twice as thick. Blow-drying curly hair can create soft, smooth curves, and limp hair can be shaped into a distinct style. Despite all the good results, you can damage your hair if you don't use proper blow-drying techniques. Here are some tips for successful blow-drying that will keep your hair healthy:

- ⇜ Apply a protective heat-styling product to towel-dried hair before you begin.
- ⇜ Always use the blow-dryer on a warm, not hot, setting and keep the dryer about six inches from your head at all times. Keep the dryer moving as your fingers comb your hair. Avoid focusing the heat on your hairline and ends because these areas dry quickly. Start at the back of your head and work up to the crown first: then forward to either side of your head.

Risko

❧ To keep your hair full and pliable, dry your hair only until it is slightly damp. Blow-drying hair until it's *bone dry* can damage your hair and leave it flat-looking.

❧ For a soft, smooth look, roll each section of hair under with a round styling brush. Don't pull hair taut—this keeps hair from curling. After you dry each section, leave the brush in place for a few extra seconds. This will set the curls. Allow the curls to cool completely before you brush and style.

❧ For instant volume,: Bend at the waist and brush all of your hair forward as you dry it. While hair is slightly damp, toss it back into place. Fluff it lightly with your fingers.

Mousse Magic

There is a magic foam called mousse—a recent development in hair care you can buy at any drugstore—that's guaranteed to give your hair more body, style, and shine regardless of its length or texture. Almost any style can be created, as mousse combines a hair spray's hold with the styling power of a gel. And best of all your hair never looks stiff, sticky, or greasy.

Experiment! Try a puff of mousse on wet or dry hair—try it in spots where you want extra control or all over to create a total look. Imagine me or yourself with short hair. Here are some terrific ways to use mousse:

❧ *To emphasize body:* Apply mousse to towel-dried hair. Bend at the waist and blow-dry hair as you finger-comb your hair forward, lifting at the roots. Use heated rollers for ten minutes and fluff.

❧ *To emphasize waves:* Apply mousse to towel-dried or dry hair—especially where you want to work in the waves. Lightly blow-dry, finger-dry, or use a curling iron to create the waves.

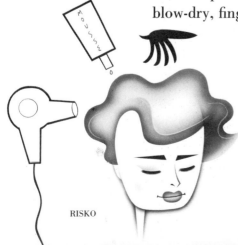

RISKO

⪢ *Fluff up short hair:* You'll need styling gel and mousse. Shampoo and towel-dry hair. To the sides of hair apply a dab of styling gel. Slick back the sides. Now comb a little mousse through the hair on top and tousle hair with your fingers. You can make it as wild looking or curly as you want. Let it dry naturally.

RISKO

⪢ *The chignon look when you've got short hair:* Shampoo and towel-dry your hair. Work a generous amount of extra-hold mousse (or styling gel) through your hair. Slick back your hair on the sides and on top so that all of your hair hugs tightly to your head. This is a great disco look. No matter how much you dance your hair will stay in place.

RISKO

Long Hair

I love my long hair because it's so versatile. One of my favorite tricks is to wind my hair around pencils and put them on top of my head! And when I'm really busy at school, what could be easier than a ponytail or braids? Here are four variations on that theme:

THE KNOT—Instead of just tying your hair back, tie it in a knot. First brush your hair back. Now part it down the middle so that it's in two sections. Cross the left section over the right section and then loop it up through the middle as if you were actually going to knot it. Smooth the ends downward and fasten with an elastic at the base of the knot.

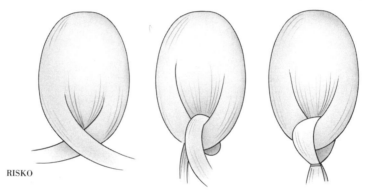

RISKO

THE TWIST—This is a simple version of the braid that looks chunky. First brush your hair back. Now part it down the middle so that it's in two sections. Gently twist each section as you cross the left section over the right section. Continue twisting and crossing until there's about an inch left. Fasten with an elastic.

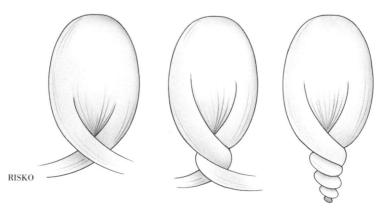

RISKO

CRAZY BRAID—This braid is loose, asymmetrical, and very sexy looking. Brush hair slightly to one side and divide into one slender section and two plump sections. Braid loosely and fasten with an elastic.

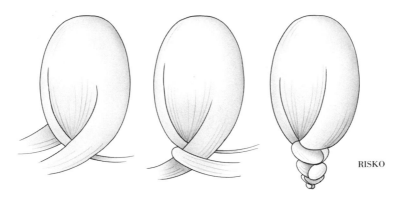

RISKO

GO BRAID CRAZY!—Give stick-straight hair a soft wavy look. I remember the time when my mom put 47 braids in my hair. While your hair is damp, make medium-sized braids all over your head and secure with covered elastics. After hair dries, take the braids gently apart and lightly brush hair into waves. (Make sure that you don't braid too tightly or you'll end up with a crimped, frizzy look!)

NAILS

I love the look of long, perfectly manicured nails . . . but the reality is, who's got the time? Colored polishes and long nails mean constant up-keep. There's nothing worse than sloppy, chipped nails. So unless you're getting ready for a special occasion, and you've got the time, I think you're best off with clean, neat nails with clear gloss as a nice finishing touch. White nail pencil will keep hands looking well-groomed, also. Try my *quick* manicure once a week for easy nail maintenance:

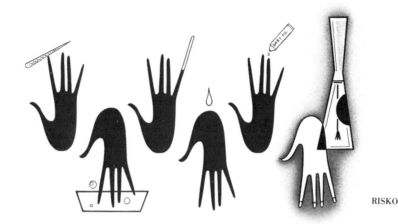

RISKO

❧ File nails into soft ovals or slightly squared shapes.

❧ Soak your fingertips in warm, soapy water for a few minutes.

❧ Dry fingers and push back cuticles with an orangewood stick.

❧ Massage a softening cream into your hands (work down each finger if time allows—a relaxing hand massage).

❧ No need for a base. Just massage a little baby oil into each nail and remove excess oil with a tissue.

❧ Apply clear polish (2–3 coats). It will last the week or longer because no one will be able to tell it's chipped but you.

For a special evening out, use the same routine but apply a base coat, two coats of color, and a top coat. Allow plenty of drying time between each coat—this is the secret for making nail color last.

CLOTHING

Chances are that you don't have the time to plan and coordinate elaborate outfits or the space to store a huge wardrobe—dorm closets are so tiny!—but you still want to dress nicely. The idea is to find your own style and build your wardrobe carefully around that style, so that no matter what you grab from your closet you'll look pulled together. If you're like me, you may find this hard to do because you like so many different looks.

Filling your college wardrobe with lots of one of a kind pieces (unusual jumpsuits, dresses, etc.) will leave you with nothing to wear day after day because these pieces usually make a statement and are not interchangeable. You wear such an outfit once and everyone goes crazy over your look. But you don't want to wear that same outfit again later on in the week. A strikingly chic, high-style look takes time and many unusual pieces of clothing. Just try putting that wild Italian sweater with the *right* pair of slacks and the *right* accessories at 7 A.M.

Remember your first year is the transition year in clothing too. So don't fret, frosh. By the beginning of year two, you'll have it down pat.

This is why I have finally arrived, by trial and error, at a basic college wardrobe that gives me everything from jeans and T-shirts to the soft romantic look—an entire wardrobe that fits in minimal storage space and travels well. It's actually a modified collegiate, preppy look (minus the Kelly green pants and bright pink shirt) with lots of interesting accessories. This is a look that's easy to put together, interchangeable, and always appears clean and fresh. At 7 A.M. I can pull on a pair of jeans, cords, slacks, or jean skirt, blindly grab a basic shirt from my closet and a sweater from my dresser drawer, and feel put together for the day.

First, Consider Your Space

At college you are usually provided with one thin closet and a couple of drawers—or if you're really lucky a whole chest of dawers. There may or may not be shelves above the clothes rack in the closet. But don't despair! With careful planning and a few inexpensive space savers you can maximize and even create more space.

DOUBLE-DECKER SHOE RACK—A double-decker shoe rack will keep your shoes orderly instead of in a scrambled pile at the bottom of your dusty closet.

CHEST OF DRAWERS—If you're lacking drawer space you can purchase one or two prefab, cardboard chests. They come in pretty colors, are inexpensive, easy to assemble, and will last the wear and tear of one semester. They're perfect for storing accessories, socks, and underwear. Usually there are a couple of enterprising juniors or seniors who make shelves that they sell on campus custom-made for dorms. One, they cost very little. And, who knows? You might meet the man of your dreams.

UNDER YOUR BED—Don't overlook the space beneath your bed. It's the perfect place for storage chests and plastic zip-up bags, which come in various sizes just for underbed storage.

INSIDE YOUR CLOSET—Multilevel pant hangers will hold at least four pairs of pants and multi-level skirt hangers with clothes pin type clips will hold several skirts at a time.

HOOKS—Plastic hooks with stickum can be placed in strategic parts of your closet and back of doors. They are ideal for hanging up bathrobe, nightgown, and pajamas or drying little odds and ends.

CLOTHES TREE (CLOTHES HORSE)—If you have the tendency not to put your clothes away daily, invest in a clothes tree. This way your clothes won't end up in a ball on the floor and you will have a great place to hang your hats. A clothes tree can also provide extra space for hanging wet towels and wash cloths.

Your Basic Wardrobe

Before I show you some different looks, I want to outline what I think are the basics. To these basics you can add as much as you have space for: more shirts, skirts, colored jeans, etc. I have planned this basic wardrobe around northeastern weather. If you go to school where it's summer all year long you'll want to make the necessary changes—shorts, more T-shirts, cotton sweaters instead of wool, rain poncho instead of heavy raincoat, etc.

JEANS AND PANTS
2 pairs denim blue jeans
1 pair of jeans in your favorite color
1 pair of brown or black corduroys
1 pair of neutral color dress pants (gabadine is nice)—optional

Needless to say, blue jeans are the standard "uniform." But for variety, I love colored jeans—red, green, purple, etc. Black or brown corduroys are also a good basic to have when you want a change. Notice that all of these basic "bottoms" will work with almost any sweater-shirt-T-shirt-turtleneck combination.

SKIRTS
1 short denim skirt or 1 leather skirt
1 midcalf skirt—a nice tweed or gabardine or, maybe a supple
        suede

Next to blue jeans a short denim skirt is the best basic bottom you can wear. Whether you put it together with a silk shirt or colorful sweatshirt, it always works. A dressier mid-calf skirt will come in handy for church, meetings with your advisor, or when you want something special for a night out, whether it's dinner, a movie or just out with HIM.

SHIRTS AND BLOUSES
1 cotton dressy blouse
4 oxford-type shirts
1 silk blouse, optional

For everyday wear oxford shirts are the best. They come in a wide range of pastel colors and interesting stripes. Best of all, they're easy to care for and always manage to look fresh. And for a special date, when you're feeling romantic, you'll want to have a pretty silk or cotton blouse to wear.

DRESSES
1 knit dress—black or a wild color that makes you feel great
1 silk dress—optional

You might want to have one or two dresses on hand. Both silk and knits store well in limited space, are easy to pack for weekends away, and can be dressed up with accessories. When in doubt, a silk dress is always right for special occasions.

SWEATERS
3 pullovers
1 vest
2 cardigans
2 turtlenecks

Have as many sweaters as you have room for. Of course you'll want to have the basic beige, black, and white, but also go for lots of color. A bright red or yellow sweater can perk you up on a rainy day when you've got long hours of studying ahead, or when you're sloshing your way from class to class.

SHOES
1 pair of boots (cowboy, to-the-knee boots, or short ankle boots)
1 pair of black pumps
1 pair of flats
1 pair of penny loafers or topsiders
1 pair of sneakers, naturally
And don't forget something for the rain or snow.

I love shoes, so it's really hard for me to say that these are all you need—who can ever have enough shoes? Maybe you can squeeze a couple more pairs under the bed!

JACKETS, COATS
1 raincoat with zip-in liner, or slicker
1 down jacket or coat—long enough to keep warm
1 oversized men's tweed jacket

A raincoat with a zip-in liner can serve the dual purpose of raincoat and cold weather coat. For really cold days a down jacket will keep

OPPOSITE
A fun dress for dates and parties—
belted, with a tie for panache.

ALBERT WATSON

*This jumpsuit combines
sweatshirt comfort,
style, and ease.*

ALBERT WATSON

*A shirtdress can be
sophisticated or sassy—
jeans aren't the only choice
for casual daytime dressing.*

DEMARCHELIER

DEMARCHELIER

ALBERT WATSON

I love the sexy allure of menswear styling.
Pearls add a touch of femininity.

Remember, separates can be mixed in any number of ways
to create a put-together, layered look.

ALBERT WATSON

Black slacks, a terrific basic, plus a cosy pullover,
have easygoing appeal.

*My wild card: this fluorescent fuchsia dress with jazzy tights
is a packable, go-anywhere treasure.*

ALBERT WATSON

Nothing beats a trenchcoat for versatility. Just throw it over anything and you're on your way.

you toasty warm and look great with your jeans. And when it comes to jackets and blazers I like to wear oversized men's tweed jackets. I wear them all the time with the sleeves rolled up, with a bulky sweater underneath (there's plenty of room), or with just a colorful T-shirt. A big tweed jacket is so versatile and there's something about the look that's casual, comfortable, and just a little bit sexy. I haunt old clothing stores and antique shops, where I find these oversized jackets at just the right price—inexpensive! Mine was five dollars to be exact.

ACCESSORIES

When you have little space and/or money use accessories to jazz up your basic look. Brightly colored hose and socks, big belts, scarves, hats, and colored gloves can really make an outfit look put together. And you can always find room for earrings, right? Costume jewelry is really the rage once again. Not too expensive, it adds the finishing touch.

SWEATS

T-shirts, sweatshirts, and sweatpants in lots of colors are a must! You'll want to exercise in them, study in them, sleep in them, and maybe even go to class in them on a day when you can't even think of getting dressed. Redesigning old sweatshirts can create a totally different look.

Ways to redesign a sweatshirt:

1. Remove cuffs and roll sleeves
2. Cut sleeves short
3. Remove sleeves completely
4. Cut neckband off

Colored T-shirts look great under recycled sweatshirts.

Day Looks into Date Looks

Your basic day-to-day look will be any combination of jeans, sweaters, shirts, loafers, sneakers, etc. The rule of thumb is that there should be at least three tops that can be worn with every bottom you have. As you add to your basic wardrobe, make sure that each piece has lots of possibilities. This way you're guaranteed not to be stuck with a lot of nice separates that don't go anywhere.

On most campuses, day looks and date looks are about the same, unless you're dressing up for a special party. Sometimes at Princeton we have chartreuse parties where everyone has to wear chartreuse. I put on chartreuse eye makeup, chartreuse fishnet stockings, a silk shirt and a black leather skirt (one of my favorite unnecessary basics). Eye-catching is an understatement!

You can convert your day look into a date look by making a few simple quick changes. For instance, if you're wearing:

❧ *denim skirt,* pullover sweater, tights, and penny loafers
   Keep the denim skirt on and change to an oversized blouse, with a jazzy belt, and jazzier earrings and textured hose will convert this to a date look.
❧ *black turtleneck,* blue jeans, and sneakers
   Keep the black turtleneck on and change to colored jeans, boots, and a big belt.
❧ *oversized men's jacket, jeans, colored T-shirt, and penny loafers*
   Keep the oversized men's jacket and jeans and change to a dressy shirt, short boots, and chunky jewelry.

You can also change your day look into a date look by adding makeup and changing your hair. Add blue liner and dark blue mascara to tired eyes. Apply mousse to short hair and style any way you want to change the look (push it back, bring it all forward). Pile your long hair on top of your head to give a soft look. Or why not try a tight chignon either high or low depending on the shape of your face.

The clothes I love most have polish, ease, and something extra to give me versatility. Accessories can take your wardrobe to the limit and beyond, when you have the basics. You have just seen some of my favorites in color to show that a minimal wardrobe can have maximum style when you've got the right essentials.

Study Looks

When it comes to study looks I go for comfort. Sitting for hours in tight pants or a short skirt is one of the worst things I can think of, so on go the colorful sweatpants, T-shirts—and of course my favorite sneakers. In hot weather I exchange my sweatpants for regular or Bermuda shorts.

What's really great about this study look is that it takes you into your exercise break. You can study for a few hours, go to the gym for an aerobics class (just take a fresh T-shirt to change into), or work out in your room and be back studying without wasting time changing in and out of clothes.

Weekend Away Wardrobe

A big part of college life at Princeton is *road trips*—we all get tired of the same haunts week after week. Several of my friends and I pack the bare essentials, pile into a car, and go visit friends at another school for the weekend. Or maybe we'll decide to visit New York City or Boston because there's a special exhibit at one of the museums, or a very exotic film that will never get to Princeton.

Of course before we leave, we are all scurrying around yelling, "What'll I wear? What'll I take?!?" At long last, I think that I've come up with the perfect weekend away wardrobe that will easily fit into a backpack or small bag.

First, wear your jeans, a nice sweater or shirt, and loafers or boots. These will be your basics. Pack a change of underwear and socks, a dressier blouse (maybe silk) and some accessories (a bright scarf and a pair of pretty flats, belts, and jewelry). If you think you'll be attending an event where jeans are inappropriate take a skirt or a soft, basic knit dress—travels like a dream. Don't forget a little ditty bag with your makeup basics: blusher, lip gloss, mascara, and maybe a brightly colored eye pencil to dress up your eyes at night. Of course you'll need to bring your facial cleanser, shampoo, and other grooming essentials. Just pack them in small, plastic travel-size bottles, and double pack them in a plastic lined cosmetic case for protection—you don't want shampoo leaking all over the place. Sling your bag over your shoulder and you're ready to go!

GEOFFREY CROFT

FEELING YOUR GOOD LOOKS

Looking good doesn't just come from your makeup and the clothes that you wear. How you feel about your looks is just as important as what you do to improve your looks. You've got to *feel* your own good looks for yourself first—what others think is secondary.

As a fashion model, a great portion of my life is centered around how I look. This can make anyone crazy at times, as you search in the mirror day after day looking for imperfections. And what if someone says or just thinks that I don't look half as good in person as I do on magazine covers? In the modeling business there's always someone who's ready to put you down, or another girl who's on her way up just as I was. If I didn't feel secure within myself and like myself, all the good looks in the world couldn't help—I'd never survive.

Looks are an attitude. People who don't feel good about their looks walk around as if they've got something to hide. Even worse, they look depressed—or angry. Their physical appearance may in fact be quite acceptable, but it's their bad *attitude* that comes through. They think, "Maybe if I had a new hairstyle, lost some weight, didn't have a long nose, whatever, I could approach my life differently . . ." Meanwhile, they let plenty of fun and opportunity pass right by. Excuses, excuses.

The girls I find most attractive, the kind of people I want as friends, have great energy. Most of the time they wear a big smile on their faces, and are constantly on the move making things happen. They don't have "cover girl" looks, but they have got a special quality, and most important, they believe in themselves. This self-assurance transcends flaws, making any physical imperfections invisible.

You've got to do whatever makes you feel comfortable with your looks. If your girlfriends are going "natural" (no makeup at all) but you don't feel comfortable that way, then do whatever it takes to make you feel your best. When you feel good about how you look you exude an energy and inner confidence that makes you sparkle. That's why even while

TOSCANI FOR *VOGUE*

cramming for exams, even if no one is around to see me, I go through my daily beauty ritual—clean face, lip gloss, blusher, brushed hair—every day. It makes me feel better about myself—and that helps give me the stamina to take on whatever project I'm facing, like memorizing a script, studying for finals, or meeting a whole new bunch of people.

If there's something you don't like about yourself, something that's hard for you to change, don't obsess. Either work at changing it, or accept it and get on with your life. At times it's harder to deal with the things you *can* change than the things you can't change. But you have to make a stab at it. I cay say this because I constantly groan about my weight, although I am getting better about it, and I know how destructive this can be.

I love to eat and I love to exercise, but for me it's a constant struggle to balance out the two. For a time I'll be satisfied with my body—I'll like the way it looks in a leotard (leotards magnify every bulge)—but by the end of the week I'll think I'm too fat. I'll start mentally punishing myself for what I've eaten during the week; how I had three helpings of salad at one meal, with all the salad trimmings, or maybe too much granola, which is one of my favorite foods and is extremely high in calories. And, even though I haven't binged on junk food, overeating any one type of food is just indulgent.

But my obsession is *my obsession*—my own little monster that only I have to deal with. I don't burden my friends with it. First of all, it's boring to hear you complain, and there's always the chance that your friends will start agreeing with you. I deal with my obsession by never giving up. I make sure to weigh myself every week. If I gain a pound or two in one week, then I work really hard to lose it the next week.

Of course there are some things that can't be changed, like your features, bone structure, height and the size of your feet—these things you just have to accept about yourself. All this depended on how wisely you chose your parents. Torturing yourself about the things you can't change can be worse than the actual problem. So focus on your positives and keep your monsters locked up!

Grades

COLLEGE IS at once a demanding and exciting experience. I really believe that what you learn and experience during these four years (and longer if you continue in graduate work) will profoundly influence the rest of your life. The studying and discipline involved provide you with a strong foundation for all future endeavors. And as difficult and tedious as college seems at times, remember that you will never again be exposed to so many ideas and so much knowledge with relatively few distractions. Indulging in learning is such a luxury!

When I finished my first year at Princeton with all A's and one B, I felt very proud of myself. Good grades means that I'm growing intellectually—and what could be more rewarding than receiving that A as a measure of my achievement? After much hard work I've reached my goal; I've met my challenge.

Of course I'm doing my best for myself first and foremost, but I'm also doing well to prove to my superiors that I can do it, that I can handle the responsibility. There's a lot of pressure on me because people are quick to say, "Look at her—she's just another pretty face—she can't do well!" I needed to prove that I had a brain and could handle academic pressure just like anyone else.

So how do I manage it? I'll be the first to admit that it's not easy—especially since I'm busy with my career. Sometimes I feel as if

I'm being pulled in twenty different directions all at once. It's not unusual for me to be studying while I'm being made up for a shoot. There are so many demands to be met and time is always limited. But instead of panicking, I look at everything as a challenge. And I love to challenge myself—I'm always trying to reach some goals that I've set for myself. And achieving good grades is one of them.

Since I always have so much to balance, I've developed lots of tricks, tips, and habits that help me get better grades. I'll be happy to share these with you, but please remember that all the clever tips in this world are worth very little without a good dose of effort from you. If you know that you've given something your best shot, then how can you feel bad? As my Dad always says, "As long as you get an A for effort, that's the A that counts!"

Making the Transition from High School to College

If you are about to enter your first year of college don't be scared. And don't spend the summer before your freshman year agonizing about whether or not you'll be able to survive all the pressures and workload of college life. College is not a terrifying monster waiting to gobble you up. It is merely a continuation of what you've spent the last twelve years doing: studying and learning. Of course there will be hefty reading assignments, big papers, and exams—but didn't you have all of that in high school too? Just remember that if you've done well enough to get into college, you'll be fine.

Academically, I didn't find my first year at Princeton any harder than my junior year in high school. In many ways I actually found high school to be harder. In high school there are lots of daily assignments and at least six hours of classes a-day. The teachers keep track of every move you make and control all your time.

But in college, it's all up to you. You don't have to attend classes and there are no daily assignments to hand in. You have to be your own disciplinarian. You have to motivate yourself to become a part of it. You can get to know your professors, attend all the classes—really get involved—or just remain a disinterested party, attending in body only. In college no one is going to care unless you care. But I promise you, the more you put into your studies, the more you're likely to get out of them.

For me probably the most difficult part of the transition from high school to college was learning to make the most of my time and making the social-living adjustments (which I'll talk about later). This is why freshman year is usually considered the toughest. There's just so much to get used to: roommates, the dining hall, being away from home, and the freedom that goes with it . . . suddenly, if you want to go out and party until 4 A.M. you can. In college there's nobody there to stop you. For the first time in your life everything isn't regimented and there's no one standing by to direct your every move. It's up to you to schedule your time and shape your days so that everything gets done. But it isn't easy being your own disciplinarian.

Day by Day—The Importance of a Good Schedule

One of the best things you can do for yourself when you first get to college is to establish a daily schedule that really works for you. Once you settle on a routine, you must stick with it. Just remember that people have different biological clocks. What works for your best friend may not work for you. I, for one, am a morning person while others love to stay up until all hours of the night. What is important is that you establish a routine that can improve your study and personal habits by being harmonious with your biological clock. Whether you are a daytime, nighttime, or anytime person, the best action you can take is to organize your time so that you make the best of your peak times. If you're a nighttime person it would be foolish to try to begin a paper at 8 A.M. If you tend to have a slump at five in the afternoon, wouldn't it be better to schedule some quiet time to listen to music rather than to try to do research in the stacks? You'll be surprised at the amount of work you'll accomplish when you listen to your body and follow your biological clock.

For me, it's up early in the morning. I shower before bed to avoid the morning rush. Besides, everybody is so zombielike in the morning. I find that kind of energy depressing. I wake up to music and allow myself enough time to get dressed and organized before I head out the door to the dining hall for breakfast.

Breakfast is very important to me because it gives me a quiet, pleasant moment before I begin my day. Usually I'll have a big bowl of granola and maybe some fresh fruit. A nice cup of *herb* tea with lemon makes breakfast complete. I love to indulge in the morning paper, or maybe I'll work on my daily list of things to accomplish for the day. But best of all, breakfast provides me with the chance to begin my day with some friendly faces—there is something very reassuring about seeing friendly faces before you dig in to the studies.

RISKO

After breakfast I go to classes and then to the library if there is time before lunch. In the afternoon I might have another class or lab, but I always try to schedule everything in the morning. This way I have all afternoon to get my studying done and maybe even squeeze in some form of exercise. If I really stick to my schedule, chances are good that I'll have my evenings free to see my friends, go to a movie, or work on a long-term project. The earlier I start my day the earlier I'm finished. Of course during midterms and finals there isn't an evening to spare except for more studying!

I don't like studying late into the night because I become so mentally exhausted by the time I go to bed that I can't sleep. And what could be worse than studying most of the night knowing that when you wake up you're going to have to start all over again?

But as I said before, everyone is different. Maybe you prefer to study most of the night, have your mornings free to sleep and then take your classes in the afternoon. What's important is that you find what works best for you, and then create a balanced schedule that you can keep. Remember to include time for exercise and leisure—going to the movies, maybe dinner with a friend. Here are some tricks that help me stick with my schedule so that I have time for *everything*.

If it's possible, always schedule your classes around your best time. If you are bright-eyed and bushy-tailed in the A.M., then morning classes are for you. If you feel incoherent until the afternoon, then you'll probably be better off scheduling your classes in the afternoon. You really want to be at your best when you attend lectures, discussions, and labs. There's so much to absorb and your professors have so much to offer.

Usually you have at least three hours of class per subject every week. They might be broken down as follows:

- ❧ meeting for one hour three times a week
- ❧ meeting for one and one-half hours twice a week
- ❧ meeting once a week for three hours

If you have a shorter attention span, or really hate to sit still for long periods of time, then you're probably better off meeting three times a week for an hour. On the other hand, I have a good friend who loves long weekends, so she prefers to have each class just once a week for three hours. This way she might be able to arrange it so that she has Mondays and Fridays free. But she also might end up with six hours of class in one day. Whatever schedule you do choose, make sure that you're not taking on more than you can handle—six hours of class in one day is a lot!

Besides my *daily list,* there is my *daily schedule* which plots my course of action for the day. On it I put my mealtimes, class times, exercise times, and study-library time. I break down my library-study time into categories. For instance, from 1–2 P.M. I will study math. From 2–3 P.M. I'll work on French, etc. When I account for my day in blocks of time, nothing—even fun time—is neglected and not one precious moment gets away. By being this aware of my time, I'm less apt to waste it.

We all know what it's like to put work off, only to have it catch up with you later on—procrastination! Avoid procrastination at all costs. The easiest way to do this is to allow yourself a minimal number of hours for studying every day. This is your time to read, review your notes or maybe put some thought into an upcoming paper. This way your work *can't* sneak up on you.

Always allow yourself enough time before your first class to get organized. This means making sure that you've got all the supplies and books you'll need for the day. You'll be able to avoid a lot of needless going back and forth if you're organized and prepared for everything. It will probably take you five minutes to do this, but in the long run you could end up saving yourself an hour or more of needless travel time.

When you are going through a heavy exam-paper period, when there isn't even one moment to spare, do allow yourself a *daily one-hour vacation.* This might mean dinner out with a close friend, going to your favorite dance/exercise class, going for a long walk, shopping, luxuriat-

GEOFFREY CROFT

Treat yourself to a daily one hour vacation.
We've all got to take time to stop and smell the flowers.

ing in a nap, or enjoying a hobby you just love. Believe me, you'll feel better and work all the harder if you've done something nice for yourself.

Make the most of your mealtimes by visiting with your friends. Mealtimes really are the perfect social breaks. You do have to eat, so why not *double your time* by using mealtimes to get caught up with your friends. That way, if you've been buried in the stacks at the library for several days, they won't think that you've dropped off the face of the earth!

If a part of your class time includes a lab (language, biology, chemistry, etc.) be aware of the lab's availability and that it involves extra work and time on your part. This way you can get your lab time in when it suits you best. Having a lab in the middle of the day can really put a dent in your schedule. I had a French lab my freshman year, but usually made my lab time early in the morning before my class. That way I was sure it got done and I didn't have to interrupt my day.

Always Have a Goal

Of course, the long-term goal is to achieve and maintain good grades, but you need daily, short-term goals to help push you along. Finishing your reading assignment for English, finishing the first draft of your psych paper or completing your biology lab for the week means that you're making some progress through that pile of work. One of my basics for achieving good grades is to keep such specific goals in mind and under control. This is why a *daily list* and *daily schedule* will really keep you moving along. I make it a game—every time I cross something off my list or schedule I'm one step closer to winning. When you accomplish your daily goals, ending your day with a crossed-off list, you have already succeeded. Remember, it's the little goals that make up the one big goal— good grades!

My favorite trick, which never fails to motivate me, is to keep a record of my semester grades for each subject inside my notebook. Every time I open my notebook I am reminded how I did in the past semester and how much better I can do this semester.

Goal setting means continual striving—never letting up on yourself. Once in a while I try to convince myself to slack off a little, loosen up. But I find that I can't have a good time unless I'm up to date on my studying and have gotten all of my work done. I'm a firm believer in keeping on top of my work all semester to avoid last-minute pressure as I face midterms and final exams. Many students "goof off" all semester and kill themselves cramming for exams at the end . . . what happens *then* if they blow it?

Developing Good Study Habits

I'm one of the lucky ones—I can study anywhere! On a train, on an airplane, or in a car, and even on a busy movie set. And it's a good thing I can because there have been times when I've been snowed under with school work and had to model for a *Vogue* cover or a fashion spread. But no matter where I am or what I'm studying, my trick is to maintain my concentration. I just shut everything out around me and focus only on the subject at hand. I've probably developed this ability because I have no choice—there are many demands on my time besides my studies. If I want to continue to get good grades as I advance in my career, I have to make the most of every moment. Of course, not everyone is forced to develop this ability. I have lots of friends who require the absolute quiet of the library stacks in order to get anything done. Another one of my friends can study only in her room with classical music playing softly in the background. I guess we all have our study quirks, but I think the following tips will help anyone improve her study habits.

First and foremost, indulge yourself with your favorite study supplies. Personally, I love stacks of legal pads. There's something about that yellow paper . . . I mean give me my lists and a stack of legal pads, and I'm a happy girl while I'm studying!

Make sure you have all the necessary study tools (pens, pencils, paper, clips, books, notes) before you leave your room. There's nothing worse than getting settled in your favorite spot, only to find that your tissue is the only thing in your pocket to write notes on.

I try to do my serious studying (exams, writing papers) *outside* my dorm. Your room should be a haven of peace and relaxation. (If you live at home the same applies.) I go to the library where talking is discouraged. There are no distractions like goodies to munch on, music blaring from the room next door, friends poking a head in to tell you their troubles or ask you about yours.

Once you've put yourself in your best study environment provide yourself with a *concentrated block of time*—let's say for four hours. Now make a quick mini-schedule: from 1–2 it's math, 2–3 it's French, 3–4 English and 4–5 psych. While you're studying French, think of French only. Don't distract yourself with thoughts about an English paper that's due or the psych quiz you've got to prepare for later. Between each subject take a 5–10 minute mini-break. You might just want to close your eyes and relax, maybe put your head on the table. A splash of cold water feels great, or step outside for a bit of air so that you can refresh yourself and clear your mind for the next subject.

When I sit down to study I deal with the least important things first, the most important things last. It's easier to concentrate when everything else is done.

Finish what you begin. If you've got 20 pages to read for biology, read it all in one sitting. Continuity is important for learning.

Some people like having a *study buddy*—another person to work with who helps them stick to the business at hand. Unless I know the material, I have a hard time studying with a friend or a buddy. I can't stand sitting passively having everything explained to me. When I know what we're studying, it can be terrific to work with someone as well-informed as I am. Together we can often arrive at a deeper understanding of the material. Also, helping someone who's having trouble can clarify the material for me.

Set priorities. If you're really bogged down with work and in a panic because you know you'll never get it all done, give your major, or the courses that count the most for you top priority. For instance, if you're a French major, and you have a lot of French as well as psychology to study, I'd study French first. Or if you have a paper due in both subjects at the same time, and you can't reschedule, do your French paper first.

I always make sure that I'm not hungry when I'm studying because there's no way I can concentrate when all I can think about is food!

GEOFFREY CROFT

Books, books, books!

A high protein snack before you begin (a hard-boiled egg, handful of nuts, a bowl of tuna fish) will give you an energy boost and satisfy your hunger.

There's a time to study and a time to STOP. The trick is to know when to stop. When you're overly tired and you push yourself beyond your limit, you're apt to get muddled. Taking a meal break, exercise break, or just visiting with friends will refresh you.

Give yourself a reward when you're done studying. (I'm always looking for the reward at the end of whatever I do!) Try a movie, read a magazine, or treat yourself to a special snack. Maybe just throwing away your crossed off "daily list" at the end of the day is enough. At any rate, you should congratulate yourself for a job well done.

When all else fails try to remember my four favorite study rules:

1. Remove all distractions and focus on the subject.
2. Work in time blocks.
3. Within a given block designate a quantity of time for each thing that needs to get done and *stick with it.*
4. Be comfortable.

Studying For Tests

First, let me say that I just dread exams. But taking a test or exam does not have to be a high-anxiety experience. Think about it. If you've gone to all of your classes and kept up with the reading assignments, chances are good that you know a lot more than you think you do. All that should be involved is reviewing what you already know. When you're preparing for a test you should not be reading a book or learning new verb conjugations for the first tme—otherwise you might be in big trouble! This is why you should keep up with your workload at all times. If you do, test-taking in general will be easier and exam week will not be so intense.

My best study trick for tests and exams is preparing *review sheets.* Review sheets can consist of a condensed version or outline of your notes which highlights the important facts; all your verb tenses and new vocabulary words, if it's a language test; all your formulas and theories, if it's a math test, etc. Sometimes you'll be given sample essay questions before the test. Writing out your answers will not only be a good review technique, but will sharpen your essay writing skills.

Review sheets really work for me because they firmly plant all the information in my mind. And with review sheets I haven't just memorized the material, I really know and understand it.

Of course, sometimes no matter how hard you've reviewed and studied, how well you've prepared, your professor might choose to pull a fast one on you just to see how resourceful you are. This happened to me on my geology exam. Before the exam, we were given 22 possible essays,

*When it comes to studying you've got to know when to stop
and take a break to refresh yourself.*

a few of which would be used for the actual exam. Well, I spent a whole week writing out all 22 essays so that I knew them backwards and forwards—I was determined to ace this exam! When I saw the exam it was a total shock. Yes, there were three of the original essay questions, but there were also five pages of multiple-choice questions for which I was totally unprepared.

If I had been in high school, I probably would have started to cry. But I thought, "Come on, Brooke—this is college—you're not the only one in this position." So I did the only thing that I could do: I randomly picked the answers as I went down the page, guessing the answers the best I could. By the end of the two-hour exam period I was laughing, literally laughing. My classmates and I were all looking at one another and shaking our heads saying, "This is ridiculous!"

Obviously this sort of thing doesn't happen often, but I have found that when it comes to taking exams always expect the unexpected. You never know when a tricky professor is going to throw a zinger at you. I often have to remind myself to keep my sense of humor. You can't always set yourself up for being perfect because in college *anything* can happen! Incidentally, I happened to choose the right answers and got an A on that geology exam.

Writing Papers

If you don't test well, writing a good, well thought out paper can save your grade. I usually do better on papers than exams. When you write a paper you can carefully plan and organize your thoughts—unless, of course, you leave your paper until the last minute. Writing a paper gives you your best chance to show what you really know.

Often you're given a list of topics to choose from. I don't analyze them or go crazy trying to figure each one out—I just choose the first one that strikes me as interesting. Then I discuss my choice with the professor so that I can get a better idea of what he wants. A consultation at this point can help get you off to a good start. At the same time, it shows the professor that you really *care*. If it's up to you to select your own topic you will probably have to do some general reading and research just to develop your ideas. Again, I suggest that you touch base with your professor. Don't think as I did at first that the professor won't have time for a lowly freshman. He will and that's what he's there for. He'll get you back on the track if you wander too far off.

Now you're ready to begin your research and get down to the real nitty-gritty of paper writing. Here are some of my methods for paper writing madness—it does get intense at times!

⤚⤛

One of the most important things to remember is always to allow yourself enough time. As soon as you know your topic and have met with your professor, begin immediately by including research time in your weekly schedule.

I use index cards for my research. Every source or reference gets a source card which lists all the necessary information for the bibliography. I give each source card a letter (A,B,C,D, etc.), and any information or quotes I get from that particular source will have the same letter on its card. For instance, source A may have ten corresponding cards because I took ten different ideas, quotes, etc., from that source. This method of research makes footnoting simple and helps you keep track of where your information comes from.

Put only one thought, idea, or quote on each card.

After I've gotten all my research done I usually write the paper in 2–3 days. I'll work on it nonstop over a weekend, or during every free moment I have. Then I put it away for a day or two and clear my mind before I tackle it again. This helps me remain objective and makes it easier for me to do any rewrites.

I try to write the paper in sections, completing each section in one sitting. For instance, when I sit down to do the outline I do the entire outline no matter how long it takes me. Or if I'm doing final rewrites, I'll do them all. When I type the paper, I type it all in one sitting. Always complete what you set out to do—this way you don't become confused and lose your train of thought.

One of my favorite tricks is to write all of the quotes in pen and the body of the paper in pencil. This way the quotes really stand out while the body of the paper can be erased and changed when necessary. I like to keep my work neat and organized at all times.

Writing a paper can be absorbing and satisfying *if you don't leave it until the last minute.* I usually find that the quality of my papers directly reflects the amount of time, thought, and energy I put into them.

Making the Most of Class Time

Your professors have a wealth of knowledge and their lectures are the time they share it. I am amazed when friends of mine or other students regularly miss classes. It's one thing to miss one or two, but I know people who miss half their classes. In the end, their grades are bound to suffer. Even if they do manage to do well, they've deprived themselves of insights and experiences that only their professors can provide.

When I go to class I'm armed to the teeth with a tape recorder, cassettes, notebook, and several pens—I want to feel that I'm ready for anything! I tape every lecture and I always take copious notes. I can never just sit there and listen. Taking notes helps me to imprint the information on my mind. When I attend big lectures, I always sit in the first row, because there are fewer distractions and I can concentrate better.

While every class varies, know that there is a time to listen and a time to participate. Large lectures are usually very intense and for listening, whereas small discussion groups mean participation is expected. Many professors consider class participation and the quality of your ideas an integral part of your grade. It's very good to talk out your ideas because it helps to make them clear in your mind. Nothing is more invigorating or illuminating than a spirited discussion, as we all share our thoughts.

One thing you might want to consider is having a "study buddy" in each class. This is someone with whom you can share your notes and ideas. He or she may have picked up on something that you didn't. If for some reason you have to miss a class, your study buddy will be there for you. A study buddy can be a valuable resource!

Establishing a Good Relationship with
Your Professor

At Princeton or other big universities, so many classes are large—especially the introductory 101 courses. Because of the enormity of the class size you can go an entire semester without ever talking to your professor, without being anything more than a student I.D. number. That's why I alway make the effort to know each of my professors. Once you get to know them, you feel less overwhelmed by their eminence and impressive knowledge. I don't know about you, but when I feel threatened I get very nervous and all churned up. Consequently, I don't do as well. But, if I know that I have a professor's support (because I've demonstrated that I'm *really* interested), everything is easier.

The best way to get to know your professors is to take advantage of their office hours, which most professors make available for student conferences. It's your best opportunity to get to know them on a one-to-one level.

Once you know your professors you can be less self-conscious with them and feel relaxed enough to ask lots of questions. Some students are so afraid to ask questions that they never learn anything besides what is said. If I'm confused, I'm the first one to show up at office hours to say, "Help! I don't understand." Not only are things made clearer, but I usually end up learning even more. But I never waste their time with idle chitchat. I only go to see them when I need help, further explanations, or supplementary reading.

If you get sick, have to miss a few classes, or just can't get that paper in on time, your professor will probably be a lot more understanding and more likely to give you the benefit of the doubt if he knows you to be a committed student.

B's Are OK Too!

Now that I've shared my favorite tips and tricks for getting that elusive A, I'm going to tell you that I think B's are OK too. In high school the A comes before all else because your grades will determine the quality of the college you get into. But college is about a lot more than good grades. The balance between the social and the academic is important, too. (Of course if you're preparing for law school or medical school, that's another story—you can barely afford to let up for a minute!) But as a liberal arts student, I don't want to be a total grind. After my first semester at Princeton, I realized that being completely academic could make a person go crazy. Everybody needs a diversion, something to clear the mind and to lighten things up—an activity, sport, something to look forward to that has nothing to do with grades.

Getting involved in the school's musical-theater group, the Princeton Triangle Club, was the best thing I've ever done for myself. It

Making my stage debut with Princeton's Triangle Club—One of my more glamorous moments with fellow student and actor Hans Kriefall.

gave me a center that I badly needed. I had to try out, had to *make it* just like everybody else. Believe me, at first I felt like a real jerk because I had to prove myself. There was even a choreographer yelling, "5,6,7,-8!!!" I got to participate in aspects of theater I never touched in my nineteen years of professional life.

By being a part of Triangle Club, I made lots of friends and was able to let loose and just have fun. I felt that I was a part of Princeton and campus life for the first time. There are times when you have to choose between putting the final "A" touch on an already "B+" paper, or going to rehearsal, hockey practice, social club, or whatever. Not all the A's in the world could give me the sense of belonging I felt when I was an active part of Triangle. If you have your A's and nothing else, the isolation you feel is terrible. That's why, if it's a question of your happiness and social well being, B's are OK too!

DAVID McGOUGH

Parents

MY MOTHER AND I have always had a special relationship. We are mother and daughter, best friends, *and* a terrific professional team all rolled into one. Mom is a captivating lady with an infectious laugh, a strong spirit, and an amazing wit. She has always been a beautiful and talented person with high ideals and an optimistic outlook on life. She was born and educated in Newark, N.J. After graduating from high school, she moved to New York and worked as a model and then as a cosmetologist before meeting my dad. Life was not easy for her as a child and she was forced to fend for herself at a very young age. Although alone, she persevered and retained her aspiring ideals. I have benefited from what my mom lacked as a young girl preparing herself for being on her own. It was important for her to give me the support that was lacking in her own life. We have been "on our own" since I was five months old when my mother and father were divorced. I'm sure that being a single parent hasn't been easy for my mom, but knowing that I depended on her totally made her even stronger. And she's always been very independent anyway. Our mutual love has always been intense. She has always given me all of herself.

When you live with only one parent, the bond is twice as close. I loved the fact that I didn't have to share my mother with anyone else. My mother's friends never invited her to a party alone, it was always, "Bring the baby"—Teri and the baby. I've only had a baby-sitter three or four times in my life. We've always had a wonderful time together. Even when

I was very young, we would go out to dinner together and then maybe to a movie. And I could be the worst brat! When she dated, I "hated" the men who took her out.

My career became an extension of our close relationship. It was something we could do together. By managing my career, she didn't have to go out to work and have a stranger take care of me. *Our* career has provided numerous opportunities for us to travel all over the world. We have been on safari, gone skiing at fabulous resorts, and taken "the cure" at various health spas where we have grunted and groaned our way through exhausting workouts while wasting away on plates of salad. The

PAUL AMATO

PAUL AMATO

*Mom and I "taking it off" together at The Greenhouse,
a spa in Dallas, Texas.*

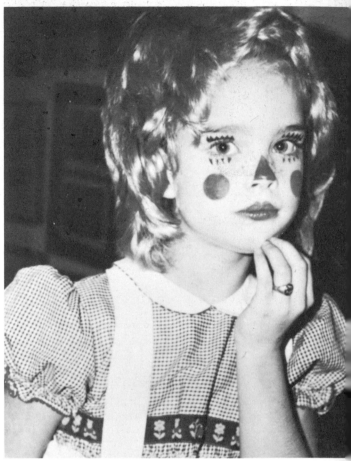

memories we share give our relationship a dimension that very few mothers and daughters have.

I'll be the first to admit that I was all consumed and all consuming as a child. Some people might think that my mother has been obsessed with my career, but I disagree. My mother has done everything in her power to protect me, to make sure my childhood was as happy as possible. I was always encouraged to have lots of girlfriends. Whenever I had to travel for my work, I always took a friend with me. My mother went out of her way to make sure I didn't miss any of the normal events and milestones of growing up. She was careful not to raise a child star—she wanted a healthy, natural daughter who could think for herself. I'm grateful that she succeeded.

If my mother was trying to hold on to me at this point in my life, I would say that there was a problem. But she's not. In fact, she is constantly pushing me out on my own. I must confess that I have the opposite problem of most girls my age: I don't want to leave. My mother keeps pushing me out of the nest. She's launching me for the big jump and I keep climbing back into the nest. The truth is that I find the leap terrifying.

I sometimes wish that I could just say, "What do adults know?" and rebel. But I'm not that arrogant. Who am I to disregard years of ex-

*Contrary to popular belief, I had a
normal childhood. One of the highlights
were homemade Halloween costumes.*

perience? The disasters our parents try to spare us from do exist. While I know I should risk more, suffer through my mistakes, or even do a version of the "Prodigal Daughter," I'm reluctant to do so. The melodrama doesn't appeal to me because I've always been so focused. And I have to admit—my mom's advice is right more often than not.

Although I was never a rebellious teenager, I am starting to grumble these days. Mom and I are having typical mother-daughter misunderstandings. I certainly don't always do as I'm told. I am tempted at times to huff out of the room when we really get into arguments, but I don't. My mother has always been very patient when it comes to hearing me out. Even when she disagrees, she lets me have my say. We communicate, and that's what is important.

As I am on my own more at Princeton, I am beginning to develop a new perspective on what I once thought were absolutes. For the first time in my life I'm telling my mother what I'll be doing for the evening rather than asking. The decisions I make aren't always the best, but they are my own.

The key to growing up is making a smooth transition from dependent child to independent young adult. The relationship you've had up until this point with your parents is bound to change. I find this to be a very strange period in my life. Right now I'm torn between doing what I want to do, considering what's right or wrong, and doing what my mother says. Help! It's not always easy being a young adult.

Being the Family Diplomat

As atypical as my family life is, there are some basics that I try to follow that should help all family relationships to run more smoothly. Most involve handling the typical parent-child confrontations we all get stuck in regardless of family structure. You might want to consider these points when you get the urge to explode. These tips should restore your equanimity during those moments of rebellion we're all susceptible to.

✄

If you want to be treated like an adult you have to act like one, especially during heated family discussion. Screaming, crying, or slamming doors is inappropriate behavior. Prove to your parents that you're ready for the responsibility you're begging for by reacting like a rational adult. This means staying calm and collected and talking things out.

Everybody is entitled to an *off day*. When it happens to one of your parents, it's not unusual for them to take it out on the nearest target—this could be you. I'm sure you've done the same to them. No matter how unreasonable they may be, grin and bear it. If you humor them, let them rant and rave without provoking a fight, chances are good that they'll be apologizing profusely before the day is over.

No matter how sticky a family situation gets, keep the lines of communication open at all times. Sulking in silence and hiding in an off-limits bedroom will only make the problem worse. Plus you'll be criticized for your immature behavior.

If you're keeping a secret from your parents because you're afraid that it's "too horrible for words," you might want to reconsider. When something is really troubling you, talk it out with someone who is close to you—and who could be closer than a parent? No one loves you more. Actually, they may surprise you and take the "bad news" well. Remember they were your age once. They understand you. So, before making yourself sick with worry, shame, disappointment, or fear, confer with someone you respect and trust.

Avoid driving if you've been fighting with your parents, or, for that matter, anyone. Anger can distract you and create a reckless attitude.

You can have a mind of your own, but you don't have to be contrary. Mindless rebellion creates confusion, hurt feelings, and anxiety for everyone, including you. Before you start, make sure the cause is worth it.

Sometimes you have to adhere to *your* principles no matter what. You'll never really know what's right or wrong unless you test it. If you hold firm to your beliefs, regardless of what your parents say, be prepared for the consequences—there could be a price to pay: loss of car

FRANKIE ZITHS © 1983

Here I am with my Mom and Dad.

privileges, a cut in allowance, or, if the issue is major, estrangement or being disinherited. Once again, make sure the cause is worth it.

What do you do if one parent says "Yes" while the other says

"No way." Before deciding to go with the parent who has given the affirmative, first consider the positions of each side. Maybe after you truly consider each side, your decision will be easier.

Dealing with Divorce

Although I have been raised in what is considered a "broken family," I have never experienced the shock that many children feel when their parents divorce. Part of the reason for this is that I was so young when it happened. I've also spent a good deal of time with my father, who was always welcome at our house. I felt neither deprived of his affections nor that he had been unfairly taken away from me. Though my experience of my parent's divorce has not been terribly disruptive, I do have friends who went through pain, trauma, and confusion when their parents' marriage dissolved. It's common to feel a real sense of loss initially. As one friend put it, "It's like my Dad suddenly died . . ."

My father has always lived within easy traveling distance from us, which enables us to visit frequently. It must be rough to have parents living in opposite corners of the world—it might mean Thanksgiving in Newark and Christmas in England. And a long-distance relationship means lots of telephone calls and letters. While nothing can compare to *in-person* visits, if phone calls and regular mail are all you have, make the most of it. Letters can be saved, to be read again and again, to console you when you're having a bad day or a blue Monday.

When my father remarried, I was thrilled because I knew it was what he wanted. His marriage also gave me an instant second family. Suddenly, I had a big sister, Diana, and a brother, Tommy, children from the new Mrs. Shields' first marriage. Later came my half-sisters Marina, Christiana, and Olympia. I love having two families.

I think I benefit from the best of both worlds. It's true that my family structure is atypical, but it really works for me. When I'm with Mom, I am an only child. I love the way I'm treated as an individual. With my father I'm just one of the kids. His concept of family is what I call the "white picket fence" school. Besides all of the kids, there are lots of pets, tennis games, and a nice surburban family home called Toad Hall. When I visit, I sometimes feel as if I'm standing in the middle of Grand Central Station—it's a totally different level of activity than I'm accustomed to.

Dad is a charming, handsome man—one of the boys, everybody's friend, a preppy grown-up. He graduated from the University of Pennsylvania where he was captain of the crew team. He adores being surrounded by his "girls." His house has a warm, friendly atmosphere. Diana and I love being big sisters to the three little ones. As much as I love visiting Toad Hall, I'm always glad to come home to my own life and my special routines. I can appreciate their way of life, and I am comfortable there, but I prefer my own.

No matter how amicable your parents' divorce is, dealing with two separate households can be difficult. Life isn't always easy when you're the kid in the middle. It's not beyond your parents to get jealous of each other over you. The fact that you're growing up and have less time to spend with either one of them can be painful.

When you go off to college, the usual every other weekend with Dad could become holidays only. Or maybe your first job makes it impossible for you to lunch with your mother every Wednesday when she's in town. You're going to have to figure out ways to accommodate both parents. There are no easy answers, but here are some *Divorce Tips* that might help you from feeling as if you are being pulled in two different directions at once.

Give the parent you visit a fair share of yourself. This means making the most of your visit. If your Mom or Dad wants to take you out to dinner, go instead of sitting in front of the TV. Spend your visit doing as much as possible together—that's why you're there. When you're down to the last few hours before leaving, don't sit with your bags packed, tapping your foot, ready to go. Eagerness to depart is insensitive and will make your mother or father think you had a rotten time. Whether this is true or not, make every moment count.

It's not unusual for parents to talk about one another to you. I think that it's better not to take sides and just listen. Chances are good that this parent just needs to get something off his or her chest.

It's very possible that you are closest to the parent you live with simply because you spend more time together. This is nothing to feel

Meet my wonderful "second" family. From right to left they are:
Baby Olympia, Cristiana, Marina, me and Diana.

NANCY BARR

Celebrating my sweet sixteen with Dad at New York's Regine's.

guilty about, but don't allow your relationship with your other parent to disintegrate. Keep yourself open during your visits—chances are good that you'll have a better time than you think.

Even if you are juggling two full households including lots of step-brothers and sisters, you've got to remember birthdays, holidays, anniversaries, etc. Besides being a nice thing to do, such thoughtfulness keeps anyone from holding anything against you. And what could be better than hearing how thoughtful you are? Tip: At the beginning of every New Year mark every date on your calendar—this way you'll never forget!

If you feel deprived because your parents are bicoastal, don't despair. Those of us who have easy access to both parents find it chaotic at times, lugging stuff back and forth as we juggle visits. It's inevitable that things get left behind!

How My Father Handled My Career

I'm closer to my father now than I was in the past, although I've always felt that I understand him. He loves his family, but he can be stubborn at times, totally inflexible. He doesn't understand my business at all, and the truth is that he has never accepted my career. I could let myself get angry about this, but I don't. Since I understand him, I think that it is easier for me to deal with his disapproval than it is for him to deal with my success.

He never wanted me to get involved with "all of this," to become a celebrity. I'll never forget doing the family picture for Christmas one year when I was about six or seven. Since I had already done a lot of modeling, I was very comfortable in front of the camera. As we all sat on the lawn, even the dog, getting ready for the picture to be taken, my Dad said to me, "No posing. No posing. I don't want you to look or act like a child star!"

I said, "Dad, we're taking a family picture and I want to look the best that I can. So I am going to smile—and don't be ridiculous!"

My father has always been paranoid that I would become a "Hollywood Girl"—whatever that is. So there has always been a conflict between us because of my career.

I've handled this conflict the only way that I can: I've humored him! I know what is right for me. Instead of fighting with him, I just go along with him. I know him well enough to realize that regardless of what I say he isn't going to change his attitude. But just as I'd like him to respect my opinions and beliefs, I have to respect his, even though I don't agree with him.

I realized at an early age that I wouldn't be able to sway him, so I've never tried. When you start trying to prove yourself to anyone, you only end up feeling exasperated and bad about yourself. I hate defending my actions and goals—it puts me in such a vulnerable position.

Since my career is a problem for *him,* not me, I just listen. I can only hope that by talking it out honestly, he can feel more relaxed about the whole situation. I think that I'm dealing with our conflict the best way that I can.

Dealing with Family Problems

Sometimes it's easy to forget that our parents are human beings too, susceptible to lots of problems. Their responsibilities can seem overwhelming to them at times, and we don't always make it easy for them.

It can happen to any of them—one day they just snap! Maybe they have a nervous breakdown, get hooked on Valium, or start drinking too much. Regardless of what it is, suddenly your world collapses, you feel as if the rug has been pulled out from under you, and there's a major family problem you have to deal with. In such a situation it's not unusual for you to feel as if your roles are reversed—you've become the parent and your mother or father is the child. You might become adjusted to this new role or you might resent it.

When I was thirteen I realized my mother had a serious drinking problem. I took on the role of parent to her child, and did I ever take good care of her. If she got drunk in a restaurant, I'd help her home. If she passed out on the couch, I covered her up. The most difficult aspect of her alcoholism was dealing with the two different people who my mother became.

In the morning, she might have been hung over, but at least she was sober. I used to say to her, "I wish I knew you only in the morning." As three o'clock rolled around, and I knew I'd be leaving school, I'd begin to panic. I knew she would be drunk when I got home. And I would get angry. As long as she didn't drink she was a wonderful, loving person, but to see her drunk was terrible. The extreme personality changes really confused me. I began to feel as if I didn't know who my mother really was. I was filled with all kinds of insecurities. I wondered, if she really loved me, how could she possibly drink? What I didn't understand at the time was that alcoholism is a disease and, as with any other disease, the people who are afflicted are sick.

Her final drinking days were increasingly difficult for me to handle as our lives became more out of control. I couldn't sleep at night because I knew that I'd be dragged out to the living room at 3 or 4 A.M. to watch television. I never knew what to expect from one moment to the next.

Mom never was abusive, but she would become furious at every little thing. Her anger sometimes became unintentionally violent. Once, she threw a plate at me which accidently hit me. Of course, she felt awful about it. And I played up the whole incident because I wanted to make her feel bad. When I did this, I realized that we both needed help.

My Aunt Lila and I, with the help of a friend, contacted doctors and counselors who specialized in alcoholism. They decided that it would be best for my mother to go away to a rehabilitative hospital. I followed their instructions, packed her a bag and told her that she would have to leave on a 5 o'clock flight. She was gone for six weeks. Being on her own, coming to terms with her problem, and helping herself was the only way she would get better. Up until that time, I had taken such good care of her that it made it easy for her to stay sick.

It was difficult for her at the hospital because she went there as "Brooke Shields' mother." But Mom stuck it out, got well, and somehow kept her wonderful sense of humor through it all. She would send me

Mom and I visiting friends.

postcards on which she had written: *Greetings from the looney bin* . . .
Having her away was hard on us both, but very necessary.

When she returned, healthy and well, I became hostile and acted
like the worst little brat imaginable. To this day, I don't understand why.
I was so unsympathetic to what she had been through and I refused to appreciate the positive changes. Maybe I wanted to punish her for all the
pain we had felt in the past. She certainly didn't need me to take care of
her anymore. All she needed was my love. At any rate, for the first two or
three weeks after she came home, I did everything I could to make her
miserable. I think that I was testing her to see if I could make her drink
again. Once secure of its not happening again, I started to appreciate our
new beginning and I was so thankful that she was well again.

I've blocked out much of what happened then. I think it's healthy not to dwell on that period of our lives because it's all in the past. When I look back at that time, I realize how much pain was involved—we were both in pain. Each of us in our own ways were victims of what is now considered a family disease. When there is an alcoholic in the house, the whole family is affected.

If one of your parents has a problem with alcohol or drugs, and it is adversely affecting your life, please seek advice from professionals. There is an organization called Ala-teen (a branch of Alcoholics Anonymous) that you can call. They'll help you in every way they can, and, if they can't, they'll refer you to someone who can. Be brave and know that you aren't alone. All problems can be resolved, but *you* have to initiate action to find the solution. If I hadn't sought help for *our* problem, who knows what would have happened to my mother and to me.

What Family Means to Me

Whether you live with one parent or both, regardless of all the ups and downs, problems, anger, confusion, and crazy moments, there is nothing like family. Think of all the good times! Summer vacations together, learning how to ride a bike with your Dad, Christmas, birthday parties, picnics. . . . And what about the little things, like being tucked in night after night, being comforted after a nightmare, or a disappointment, or just knowing that you're not alone. For every negative family situation, I can think of at lest ten positives.

Anyone anxious to be out the door and on her own will soon realize how good she had it. It's amazing how we take all the love and support our parents have given us over the years for granted. They have been our advisors, our support system—it's because of their guidance and caring that we are healthy young adults ready to be on our own.

No matter how much you come to love someone else, chances are good that no one will ever know you or love you like your family. The tie that you have with them, for better and worse, has no end and the lifeline between you will go on forever. No matter where I live or what I ultimately become, I know that I *can* go home again. Yes, grown-up Brooke is different from little Brooke—but I am still Brooke and I'll always have a family.

DEMARCHELIER

Clowning around with some of my high school friends.
From left to right, from the bottom, they are: Tia Goldberg, Lisa Canino,
me, Gigi Sanchez, Mara Cohen, Diane Coleman, Missy Sherman.

Friends

WHEN I FIRST ARRIVED at Princeton, everyone was very cool toward me—as if they'd agreed "Let's not talk to her so she doesn't think we're star struck like everybody else." I also had roommate problems, which I've since discovered is not at all unusual for a freshman. At the time, though, it seemed a total disaster. I felt like a real outcast.

People were trying to be nice and not bother me, but I felt isolated and alone. Since they didn't approach me, I had to go out and make friends. I'm just as insecure as anybody else when it comes to reaching out and exposing myself. People were very responsive and although it took time they realized I was just like anybody else who wanted friends and needed to belong. It was worth the effort because I've formed the most solid friendships I've ever had.

It's never been hard for me to make friends, but because I'm away so much of the time, keeping them is a harder job. Constantly being in the public eye doesn't help either. One of the ways I cement my friendships, while being away, is to take a friend with me if her time permits. But there are always friends I leave behind and I can't help worrying that they're going to forget me. Every time I come back, I'm afraid that they'll ignore me. Of course, this is ridiculous because they never do. But my paranoia still exists. I return worrying: "Will my friends still like me?" "Will I still fit in?" I love it when they say they've missed me!

Friendships are our lifelines and our support systems. What could be more difficult than being in a new environment full of strange faces? Not only has the comfort of familiar surroundings vanished; suddenly all your old friends are gone too and you've got to start from scratch.

I really thought I would *die* my first semester at Princeton because I was so lonely and homesick for my friends and family. To make matters worse, I was also putting enormous pressure on myself to do well. It was a real catch-22. I didn't feel I could let go and have fun until I was academically acclimated, and yet I couldn't get past my emotions to sit down and study.

I was so miserable and confused that I couldn't get energized to enjoy anything or anyone. All I could think about was how much I wanted to be home. Often I'd break down and go home for the night (an easy thing to do since I live about one and one-half hours from Princeton). I'd have to leave at 6 A.M. the next morning to make my first class. I'd cry at home, I'd cry at school; I felt like such a baby. I must have called my mother at least six times a day, pleading, "I want to go home. Please come and get me!" She was strong for the both of us and helped me survive. We had many lunches in New York where I would just sit there whimpering, "Mom, I can't go back." She would calmly and patiently say, "Look, analyze it. You know deep down inside that if you don't you'll never forgive yourself. All of this will pass. And tomorrow is another day. You know you love it there and you will make friends." As much as it hurt her to see me like this, she didn't give in.

I was so lonely during that first semester that on mornings when I wasn't driving to school from home I would get up early to do aerobics with the teachers and Princeton employees at the gym. It reminded me of when I started high school. The only place I would sit at lunch was at the teachers' table. And that did nothing to improve my rapport with my classmates. I felt comfortable with the employees and teachers—but when it came to my own peers, I was insecure. That first semester I cried a lot, studied a lot, went home a lot, and exercised a lot—it wasn't a very satisfying way to live. But I did stick it out, though, and now I'm glad I did!

I've come a long way since then—it really did get easier. Now I've got a bunch of friends and feel a part of the campus scene. I made some friends in the Triangle Club, the musical-theater group, and others in social clubs. I've even got a nickname: *Monster.* My girlfriends call me *Monster* because I'm always the first one up in the morning; and I'm always organizing everything, making plans for us, and anticipating any conceivable problem.

The only thing you can do when you're new, alone, and afraid is to hold firm, knowing that in time you will meet people and make friends. Try spoiling yourself with your favorite things: indulge in movies, new records, and maybe a new outfit. Just go easy on yourself and *allow* yourself the time that everybody needs to adjust to a new environment.

But also be aware that you'll have to give 150 percent sometimes and really make the effort because you can't count on people coming to you. This might mean sticking your neck out and doing something terrifying like trying out for a sports team. For me, it was getting up my nerve to audition for Triangle. Once I did and became actively involved, the barrier was broken. People finally began to believe that I was like any other student.

The Reality of Roommates

There's a preconceived notion that you'll be best friends—"sisters" for life—with your college roommates. The reality is that it just doesn't happen. I fell into the trap, and, like most kids, expected my roommates to become my best friends immediately. I imagined that we'd tell our secrets during late night talks over a bowl of granola, share our clothes, and cry on each other's shoulders when we didn't think any of us could tolerate one more moment of studying—just as I'd seen in so many movies.

It didn't happen that way for me. In fact, we didn't even become

This is the best way to travel incognito.

It didn't happen that way for me. In fact, we didn't even become friends. The reality was that we were four different people who had very little in common. We just went our separate ways.

Though there are girls who become very close to their roommates freshman year, don't think you're weird or that there's something wrong with you if it doesn't happen. Remind yourself that you didn't pick your roommates. They were randomly selected for you.

Whether you have a single roommate or a roommate and two suite-mates like I had my freshman year, not getting along with your roommates is not the end of your college career. It just means that you'll be forced to look elsewhere for a circle of friends, which in the end could work to your advantage because you'll be exposed to many more people. Remember that there are other girls living next door, down the hall, and probably above and below you—it's really not as hopeless as it seems.

Of course, you still have to *live* with your roommates. This means cooperation on everyone's part. If one of you is a late-night worker, while the other is an early riser, you'll just have to be considerate of each other. Try to talk openly and objectively about any other individual needs and make compromises whenever possible. It's best to avoid any unnecessary friction whenever you can, and to talk things out before they get out of hand. It's the little things in these situations that can snowball into major fights—like who's using the shower first or whose turn it is to vacuum this week. At all times, try to respect each others' rights, need for privacy, and space. Borrowing without asking first or having your boyfriend there every evening when she comes in are both intrusions on her space. If you're confused about what's right or wrong, put yourself in the other person's place. How would you feel if the situation was reversed? Just because you're not friends doesn't mean you have to become enemies!

Getting involved in social clubs, sororities, and athletic activities are good alternatives for making friends. In high school you were probably involved in student government, language clubs, or maybe you worked on the school newspaper. Chances are good that through these activities you made a lot of friends—the same applies in college. Putting yourself in social situations where interests are shared is a great way to meet people. Also consider church and religious groups that are not necessarily within the college sphere.

Clubs and Cliques

Instead of fraternities and sororities at Princeton, we have dining clubs. These clubs are wonderful old houses where you eat your meals and have social gatherings, but you don't live there. Some of the houses are coed, and some are exclusively for men or for women.

Joining one of these clubs provides a student with a fun place to eat and can give her a real sense of social belonging. For me, going to my dining club for a half-hour lunch without a book in my hand relaxes me—it's a wonderful respite from a busy day and a great place to "hang out" when I feel down. Having lunch with my friends enables me to approach the rest of the day with more energy.

To become a member of any of these clubs you must "bicker"— these are intense interview sessions that take place every day for a week. During this time you are expected to get to know as many people as possible to show your interest in the club. At Princeton, the selection process involves a unanimous vote for membership. I've been told that this process is similar to what's involved in joining sororities at other schools.

If you join a social club, be careful not to focus only on other members. It's so easy to get caught up in cliques. It's great to belong, but keep yourself open to other opportunities that might also enrich you. Clubs and cliques can become very confining and their exclusivity can narrow your point of view. I know that I want to meet and experience as many types of people as possible and still make time for my old friends. Abandoning old friends as you seek out the new could leave you with nothing in the end.

One major drawback to clubs and cliques is that not everyone who tries out gets in. It's painful when you want to be accepted by a particular group and you're not. Or what if you are accepted, but your close friend isn't? You have to consider all possibilities if you're going to try out for a club. You have to be ready to accept disappointments. Rejection is tough. There's not much you can do about not making the social club of your choice except to view the situation philosophically. Though this thought might seem a cliché, some things just aren't meant to be. Try not to be too hard on yourself and don't get trapped in negativity. If it's not in the cards, you'll just have to get over the disappointment and get on with your life by setting new goals for yourself.

If you are not accepted into a club, sorority, clique, or whatever, there are some things you *shouldn't* do. Don't banish yourself from all friends and activities or lock yourself in your room—there's no need to be ashamed! And don't change your look, hoping that you can become somebody else. Stay just as you are, but turn to other groups of people for support. I believe that there's something for everybody somewhere. Maybe it just wasn't the right place for you to be. The trick is to find the group that will appreciate and support all of your wonderful assets. Maybe you weren't accepted because you were trying too hard—trying to be someone other than who you really are—and lost touch with yourself in the process.

A Friend in Need

Parties and fun aside, I rely on my friends primarily for the emotional support of knowing that they are "there." It's a very good feeling to know that someone will be there for you if you need her, and, of course, you're there for her too. Friendship often involves sacrifice, like putting down your work to listen to *her* problems. Unfortunately, problems don't ever come at convenient times. There's no question about it—you have to give a lot to keep friends. But the more you give and the greater your effort, the richer the friendship will become.

Friendship needs a lot of time and patience if it's going to develop into something strong and lasting. But the time it takes is well worth it because the trust and affection that you share can last a lifetime. My friend Lisa and I have been *working* on our friendship for five years and we still learn new things about one another every time we get together. Since we go to different schools, we sometimes get a little jealous of each other's relationships with new friends. Even with our ups and downs, we've always shown each other patience and understanding—this is what friendship is all about.

"Hangin' out" with my close friend Lisa.

All of Me

Now that I'm comfortable and familiar with school, I realize that Princeton is just one tiny part of my life. I have friends in every area of my life and Princeton is one of the most important.

I don't deny that I am different from the average college student. My career has given me experience that most people don't have the chance to develop until they leave college. When I work on a movie set, I'm constantly made aware of major problems that involve money and jobs. Making a film is such a big undertaking. And then I return to school and see people getting upset about things that seem so small. I do so as well but always have to gain perspective.

Having some sort of overview can help you to keep everything in perspective. Try reading the newspaper or a weekly news magazine regularly. Staying informed about what's going on in the real world can help you to keep a sense of humor about life on campus. There's a great big world out there that you shouldn't lose sight of. When collegiate life gets you down, it's a relief to realize that your everyday concerns are trivial in the great scheme of things. It works for me.

Fortunately, my current roommate and I have much in common. Born in Norway, she has been brought up in Europe and America. She is well-traveled and has been exposed to many of the realities of the adult world. Sometimes, the things we and our friends at Princeton get upset about seem so ridiculous—I thought that the pettiness would end in college and we would be adults. Our experience does not make us feel superior to the others. In the end, it doesn't matter where you come from or how you've grown up, we all experience the same anxieties.

I try to appreciate each different group of friends, not to judge, and to mix with each of them as best I can. I get phone calls from friends saying "We never see you anymore . . . How come you were with such and such . . . Why haven't you done this . . ." and on and on because they feel neglected. It's difficult to keep the proper balance in my life. And the demands at parties can be overwhelming. Recently, at a huge lawn party

Roommate Cecelie and I on our way to class.

given by one of the social clubs, there were circles of kids on the lawn. I had a few good friends in each group. As I moved from group to group, I felt very uncomfortable. The groups didn't know one another and I became frustrated that they weren't mixing. It was enough to make me crazy. At Princeton, it didn't take me long to realize that I have to do what I want to do and be with whom I want to be. I can no longer worry about what everyone will think. I need to do what will make me happy and keep a part of me to myself. I have many good friends with whom I love to spend time.

Often the need for friendship can overwhelm your life. Friends can start taking over. That's why I think that one of the most important aspects of friendship is always to *keep your person for yourself.* We all want to be liked and admired by our friends, to be popular, because it makes us feel good about ourselves. But sometimes you can like a person (or group) so much that you find yourself taking on characteristics that will appeal to your friends. When a girl you've always admired starts showering you with attention, you might find yourself suddenly dressing like her, talking like her—and before you know it your individuality starts slipping away.

Always keep your center and hold onto your self. You can love your friends and help your friends, but you've got to be what you are. If you change into someone you think your friends will like better, then you've lost yourself. And think of the energy involved in trying to be "that person" all of the time—no one can keep up that level of charm forever! As

Here I am with some of my Princeton pals:
Sally Landolt, John Hoyt, Lixy Paradise.

JUDY BURSTEIN

much as I need and love my friends, I don't ever want to become any-one's clone or to become too absorbed by my friends. I know a strong, solid core is necessary to accomplish what I want in life.

Friends for Now

I realize that a part of growing up is accepting that my friends will change, just as I change. Going to college, developing a career, getting married—all of these life processes take us to new places and bring new people into our lives. As we grow and mature, some of our friends will grow with us, while others will grow in a different direction. It happens all of the time: You go away for the summer and when you come back you and your best friend are suddenly strangers. She seems "different" to you and all the things you once shared now seem inconsequential. Your friendship is no longer the same. As painful as it is, it's time for you to let that friend go. The process of making films compresses this experience and has taught me an important lesson.

For me, one of the most difficult aspects of making a film is deal-ing with the intense friendships that develop and the inevitable parting of the ways that comes when the film ends. When I make a film, the crew, other cast members, and I become one big closely-knit family as we work. Usually we are on location, which basically means that we're to-gether 24 hours a day. We work long hours together and afterwards we play and relax together.

Sometimes the friendships and interrelationships that develop be-come so overwhelming that it's a relief to be on camera acting. While I'm acting I can cry, scream, or laugh hysterically, but I know that I'm safe. I can experiment with a range of feelings and then leave them behind when the scene is over. These feelings are real only in the context of the film and nobody can hold me to them. But with the crew and other cast mem-bers, everything I feel is real. These are people that I've stayed up with until dawn, waiting for the right lighting and the perfect shot; people that I've laughed with over hot cups of coffee at 3 A.M. I feel so close to them

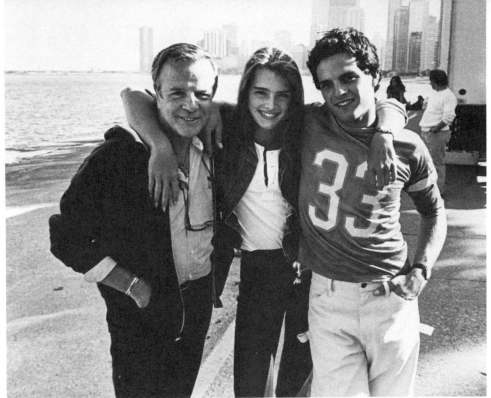

On the Endless Love *set with director Franco Zeffirelli
and Martin Hewitt . . .*

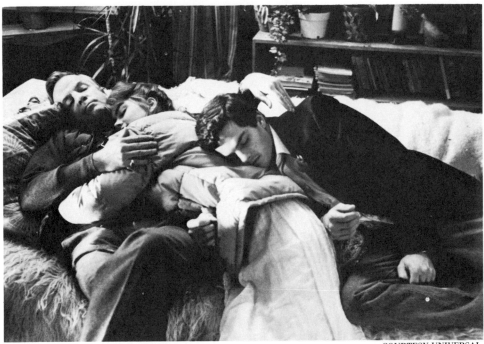

and becoming close friends with Franco and Martin on the set.

Taking five with some of the crew from Blue Lagoon.

all and I mean everything I say. I've listened to their problems and they've listened to mine—in a very short period of time we've become very good friends and have shared a great deal.

And then the movie is over; the final cut, the last take. Everybody packs up and goes their own way. It's so sad. As I leave, I can hear myself telling one person that I love her or another that if he ever needs a friend he could count on me. Although I sincerely mean everything that I say, as we disperse and go our separate ways, I realize chances are good that we'll never see one another again. It really hurts me to know this. As far as I'm concerned, in the movie business it's not the "drugs" that will ruin you—it's all the emotions! True friends will prevail.

When I was filming *Wet Gold* between my freshman and sophomore years, I noticed a guy on the crew who looked very familiar to me but I couldn't place him. One day, as I went down into the galley of the crew boat, I saw him and said hello.

He looked at me and said, "You don't remember me, do you?"

"Were you here on the first day of shooting, gone for production, and now you're back?" I asked.

"No, I was the cameraman on *Pretty Baby,*" he replied.

"My God," I thought, "this is Mike McGowan, the camerman that I haven't seen since I was eleven years old." I couldn't believe it!

Filling in my flustered silence, he said, "It's so strange, isn't it? I still have the Polaroid of the two of us on the camera dolly eight years ago and now we're saying hello as if it were yesterday."

As I go out on my own and spend more time away from my family, all personal relationships are important to me—friends are vital! That's why it's so hard to say goodbye. I've learned to be thankful that we had the close time we did for as long as we did. With my movie friends, I can only hope that we'll work together again someday.

Barbie and Ken go to the prom.
Ted McGinley of The Love Boat *was my date.* (April '83)

Boyfriends

I'LL BE THE FIRST to admit that intimacy scares me right now. The last thing that I need or want at this point in my life is a serious relationship. Having a boyfriend means an added commitment for which I'm not ready. I'm not willing to be distracted from my goals or to limit myself while I'm so young.

For some girls, college may be the last stop before marriage, which is fine, if that's what they really want. But I want to feel established in my career before I start thinking about marriage and children. That's why I look at this period of my life as my time to focus on myself. As my experience broadens and deepens, I will have more to contribute to a relationship. When I am comfortable with myself and my achievements, I will be eager to build a strong and rich attachment to the right man.

Young women today have so many opportunities to consider, so many options. We are in the perfect position to pursue every dream and fantasy—become whatever we want to be. We no longer have to follow in our mothers' path. The old threat "You'll be an old maid" doesn't apply to our generation.

I know that I'm not going to jeopardize my career to rush into a relationship. I believe that it will all fall into place when the time is right. Before I start sharing my life with anyone else, I've got to take care of me. So for now, I'm not planning on getting too involved with anyone. While I'm at school, I want to enjoy dating, to keep my relationships platonic, to date a number of men so that I can be exposed to all types. This way, when I am ready to have a relationship, I'll know the type of man with whom I want to share my time or even the rest of my life.

What My Virginity Means to Me

I'm willing to admit that I'm a virgin because I feel so strongly about it. Believe it or not, I'm not as unusual as you might think. Like me, there are plenty of college girls who don't want to be bogged down with demanding involvements or have to be concerned with the emotional or physical consequences of sex. For the time being, we're more concerned with getting ahead and making the most of our creative potential.

I do have girlfriends who confide, "Oh Brooke, have I got something to tell you!" as their faces blush scarlet. Or they'll write letters saying, "Fell in love. Will explain later . . ." And that's OK because this is a personal decision that every girl comes to at a different point in her life. Because of feelings I've had in the past, I realize this could create a conflict. That's when I think about the future. We all have individual needs, expectations—what's important is that *you* decide when you're ready for sex.

Though I am sexually inexperienced, I'm as aware as any other young woman of the power of body chemistry. I've felt that physical attraction. But I know that it doesn't always mean love, and love is what I want to wait for. I don't feel the need to experiment. I'd rather just wait until I'm ready to have a serious relationship. For me sex and love go together—I just can't imagine having sex without an intense involvement. So far, I haven't felt strongly enough about anyone to give them all of me.

My feelings about love derive from my religious upbringing, which is a very positive part of my life and provides me with a strong base on which to focus. Nowhere in my busy schedule do I find the tranquility and peace of mind that I do when I attend church every Sunday.

My religious beliefs have provided me with a solid grounding of consistency, a definite sense of right and wrong. I need the objectivity that religion provides. Religion was not crammed down my throat, threats of eternal damnation waved before me if I didn't believe. I was presented with the universal rights and wrongs, *without the guilt,* and have found them to be a positive, necessary structure for my life.

If anything has been stressed in my religious upbringing, it's being aware of the consequences of my actions. But it's very hard not to be impulsive at this age, especially when it comes to sex. Passion doesn't understand religious virtues. That's why it's so important to consider all aspects of what we are about to do, before we do it.

Playing the Field

Professionally speaking, I know some real hunks: Christopher Atkins, Michael Jackson, John Travolta, Tom Selleck, and someone more my own age, Bob Hope, to name just a few. Dating or working with these men is great fun, but I also date regular nice young men. This isn't always easy. Some men are frightened by my celebrity, others consider it a challenge. The latter type often push too hard.

There are some men who are just obnoxious. One man whom I dated briefly during my freshman summer wouldn't take no for an answer; he kept calling and harassing everybody at my house. He couldn't understand how I could turn him down. His arrogance was amazing. You don't have to be a celebrity to attract a man with this sort of attitude. If you find yourself in such a situation, just be patiently firm.

One August, when I was in California, I dated a young man once before leaving. When he asked, "When can I see you again?" I told him not until Thanksgiving. I wasn't planning on returning to California until then. The minute I got to New York a huge bouquet of roses arrived with a note: *Due to the influx of turkeys, Thanksgiving has been changed to September 1st.* It was a clever way to try to get me back to California but it didn't work—I had to start school. I did appreciate his creative attempt. Though this sort of attention might seem enviable, I can't stand the final awkward confrontations or the hurt involved.

Hunks in assorted sizes.

FRANKIE ZITHS © 1983

But regardless of all the dating problems involved when you're a celebrity, I still need just to date like any other young woman. I need to find out what different men are like, so I constantly push myself to be more open and responsive to new situations. I think having an active dating life is the best way to do this because it allows you to stay virtually unattached while providing you with lots of opportunities to learn about men.

I like playing the field because it leaves me open to so many new experiences. Life can get rather exciting when lots of men are calling you, each one offering a different activity. Since you're not tied down to anyone in particular, you can date and enjoy all of them guilt-free!

The best way to avoid getting involved is by not seeing any particular man too often. If I'm casually dating someone and it's obvious that he's more interested than I am, I allow him the "three-date maximum."

Out on the town on a group date.

Three dates seems to be the amount of time needed before most young
men cross the line from friendship to romance.

One of the safest ways to stay uninvolved while enjoying male
company is to go on *group dates.* A group date can be anything from getting a pizza to going to the movies, or dancing at a club. When you go on
a group date, you have the advantage of being with several different men
at once and you're surrounded by your girlfriends for moral support.
(Just be careful not to flirt too much with somebody else's date!) Dating
should be lots of laughs, a release from all the pressure you're under. I
love it when a group of us go out to dinner and then for a night of danc-

BRIAN QUIGLEY

*I love a night of dancing—off come the calories
and nobody gets too intense.*

FELICE QUINTO

At the sock hop, put on your dancing shoes and go!

ing. We all dance with each other. We work off calories and nobody gets too intense—we're out for a good time.

Another dating option to consider are the men at different schools. Traveling to other schools for weekends guarantees you a certain amount of freedom. Your time with a particular man is limited. By dating men at other campuses, you are left free to focus on your work when you're at school. Why not date as many men as you like—on or off campus?

Where Do I Meet Him?

A major concern for most college girls is where to meet men. It's really not a problem if you put yourself in the right situations. You can make it known that you're available without appearing too forward.

If you spend most of your time studying, take an inventory of the library. Sharing a study table with an interesting looking man could lead to a cup of coffee together and maybe an invitation for Friday night.

If you like adventure, and you're not afraid of the unknown, why not try a blind date? You could end up with a disaster or a dreamboat. Or someone in between. Girlfriends at other schools can fix you up with men they know or maybe your roommate's boyfriend has an interesting friend. While there is a certain amount of risk involved, blind dates can be fun.

Of course there are always lots of men at mixers and social clubs—so put on your dancing shoes and go! Don't feel awkward waiting to be approached. Remember, it's the eighties—girls can ask too.

Turning Off the Sexual Pressure . . . How to Say No When He's Saying Yes

I am at a turning point in my life. I'm in the process of establishing adult values, my own set of rules. I'll be the first to admit that my feelings change every day as I experience new situations. Regardless of what

TOSCANI FOR *VOGUE*

conclusions I reach, I do know that *I'll never do anything that I don't feel right about.* Too many girls compromise themselves sexually because they want to be liked. Dealing with peer pressure can be difficult, especially when you're away from home. There are no parents to control you and the rules at school are lax. No one is going to tell you when to come home or what you should do. The responsibility of these decisions is clearly yours.

We've probably all been on those innocent dates that have turned into wrestling matches—simple necking in the car, that's turning into more, or the weekend-away date who expects you to spend the weekend in his room. I'm always amazed at how some men manage to twist things around so that suddenly you're the one feeling guilty because you said "No!" The only thing you can do in such a situation is to take control by holding firm to your values. Don't be afraid to tell your date what you want. Here are some suggestions to help get you through those awful moments of awkward confrontation, when your date wants more than you want to give:

- The first thing to remember is that you don't owe anyone anything.
- Always ask yourself what you want and what you think is best for you. Be honest about your own needs and desires. Don't let low self-esteem make you discount the importance of your feelings.
- If you feel uncomfortable about something that you're about to do, chances are good that you're not ready for whatever it is that's about to happen.
- Be firm about your decision. If you give in to something for which you're not ready you'll have to deal with the emotional consequences later. And maybe more.
- Any boyfriend who demands sex from you before you are ready is not the right boyfriend for you. And don't let him trick you by making you feel guilty or weird because you're not willing to go along with him.
- If the situation gets out of control and you just can't cope, remember that you can always leave. He won't hate you. You'll probably gain his respect.

Making a quick getaway for a weekend.

DEMARCHELIER

It's not always easy to say no when he's saying yes —with Endless Love *co-star Martin Hewitt.*

❧ For weekends away, make your sleeping arrangements before you leave. This is your guarantee that you'll be sleeping alone. If you don't have a girlfriend to stay with, ask him to make the arrangements. Just make sure that it is clear where you'll be staying before you arrive. If he insists on you sharing his room, you don't have to go.

❧ Weekends away are riskier becaue you're on alien turf. If you're nervous about going alone, take a girlfriend with you and ask your date to arrange a blind date for her. This way you'll definitely have someone to share a room with and you can provide one another with moral support and double your fun too.

❧ The best way to avoid confrontations is to avoid the places where they usually happen. Keep your date *public*. Concerts, movies, campus theater, and dinner out are all safe dates. Going to his room to hear his old record collection is leaving yourself open to unwanted advances.

Dancing and Romancing While the World Is Watching

It's very difficult for me to have a romance, or even to experiment with romance, because I have very little privacy. The press loves to play matchmaker, linking me with every man I'm seen with whether or not he's eligible. I suppose this is one of the reasons I'm very sensitive about public displays of affection. I get very uncomfortable if my date gets too "touchy-touchy" on the dance floor. Now that I've come of age, every move that I make is scrutinized and taken seriously. I've earned a good reputation, one that I'm very proud of, and I'm not going to let a few careless evenings ruin my public image. I'll admit that I need to open myself up more and take a few chances—but I can't afford the consequences.

I cherish my time at Princeton, because I am able to live a somewhat normal life there. Princeton is a closed, sheltered world where it's safe to experiment. On campus, I'm treated just like any other student—it's such a relief to go about my business without the usual hassles.

When I'm traveling or in New York, I count on my mother to chaperone me, as any manager would, and to be my buffer from the hungry press and fans. People think that she never lets me alone, but they forget that it is almost impossible for me to go anywhere in public without drawing attention. I rely on Mom to maneuver me in and out of difficult public situations. If my mother is with me, it's because I want her there. She never comes if I want to be alone.

Fears, Fantasies . . . The Man of My Dreams

When I was younger, I used to lie in bed at night thinking, "Oh my God, my husband isn't out there. I'll probably never fall in love." So many of my friends were "boy crazy" and I just wasn't. I was afraid I wasn't normal.

Now that I've matured, I look forward to being deeply in love. Whereas I used to be afraid that I wasn't capable of love, what scares me now are all the possibilities—how do you know if he's *the one?* I don't believe that true love happens only once—and can't imagine how you make the leap to commit your life to someone. I wonder if my needs will change as I go through different life stages? Until I come to terms with my own confusion, I know that I'm not ready for a serious relationship. But, I can still have my fantasies . . .

Men fantasies—most of us have them. My girlfriends and I used to talk about how we would like to spend a week with Mel Gibson on a desert island. Hmmm, now *that* would be interesting. And we would fantasize about movie-style romances and fabulous wealth, and all the pleasures that both would bring.

But in reality, when I'm ready to settle down, I want to meet a man who can love me for me. In a relationship I want to be just Brooke. Some men whom I date have a problem with who I am. They are usually uncomfortable, unable to handle the situation. These are the men that I never date again. They all want to be "the one," to be my first serious relationship, and they usually have lots of advice about what I should do with my life, my emotions, and my body!

I want a man who can forget about "Brooke Shields" and who is willing to focus just on Brooke. The man of my dreams is someone with whom I will always feel comfortable and who is not too impressed by what I do. I want to be helped when I need it, but I also want my independence and freedom. I don't ever want to feel controlled or possessed but I want to feel protected.

Men who are "too nice" are boring. What could be worse than someone "yessing" everything you say. Give me a man I can fight with, who's not afraid to say what he feels, or worried about what I'm going to think, and who really knows how to make up when the fighting is over!

I don't think that any woman should ever have to settle for second best. There's no need to be desperate to have a boyfriend—no one should feel that kind of pressure. Getting to know many different types of men will help you define what you want and need in a lasting relationship. In the meantime, have fun and get on with your life. If you do meet the man of your dreams during college, terrific! If not, chances are good that *he'll* be there waiting for you, somewhere along the way, and a good relationship will evolve naturally.

ALLAN S. ADLER

I was honored to receive The People's Choice Award for
Favorite Young Motion Picture Actress.

Career and Success

GRADUATION from high school, starting college, going for your first real job—these are exciting, "first-step" moments in our lives! Although we are fresh, educated, and ready to go, we are all scared to death.

Remember that proverbial question, "What do you want to be when you grow up?" Once you graduate from high school, you're that much closer to living the answer to that question. If you did well in grade school science, your parents had you pegged as "doctor material." If you were always hamming it up at family gatherings, you probably heard, "She'll be a great actress." And what did you think? Maybe you *always* knew and you're in premed right now. Maybe you went from "nurse" to "teacher" to "violinist" and now you're getting a liberal arts education or starting your first job.

Regardless of how nervous you are about your future, whether or not you know what you want to be, now is your time to investigate. Experiment, take chances, and expand in every direction that you can. The more you know and the more to which you expose yourself, the easier it will be to make career decisions.

Don't feel that you have to enter college with a firm career goal in mind. You've got plenty of time to explore all possibilities—this is what college is all about. Choosing a career is a decision you don't want to rush.

MAUREEN LAMBREY © 1978

Relaxing on the set of Pretty Baby.

Pretty Baby

When I was twelve years old, I decided that I never wanted to make another movie again. I had just finished filming Louis Malle's *Pretty Baby*, a movie about a little girl who is raised in a New Orleans brothel where her mother was the "leading lady." When she is thirteen, she is initiated into the business.

As we began promoting the film, I experienced my first taste of how cruel the press could be. They distorted every aspect of the film and tried to make it sound as if I was a child being forced to do something against my will. No matter how often I said, "Yes, I'm happy and I want to do this," they continued to twist everything I said. I had just made a film, which is a wonderful thing in itself, and I was so proud of myself. But my feelings of pride and success were ruined by the hideous portrayal of my mother by the press. To read that my mother, whom I look

FRANCIS ING

All dressed up and nowhere to go.

PHOTOGRAPH BY RICHARD AVEDON

up to and love more than anything, was a horrible, pushy woman was a shocking experience.

I felt a real responsibility to prove that I really enjoyed making films (this was my second) and that I was not a victim of my mother's ambition. Despite my protests, nobody listened—nobody wanted to take a twelve-year-old seriously. And if they did listen, they assumed that I must have been preprogrammed with answers, incapable of original thought. The press continued to twist and recreate the truth. I recognize now that sensationalism makes better copy!

The worst part of this ordeal was that I didn't understand how people could be so mean. My mother and I were being personally attacked. As far as I was concerned, working with Louis Malle had been an extraordinary experience. I had played a part in a very fine movie. Though I had done nothing wrong, I felt that I was being punished.

When we took the film to the Cannes Film Festival, the coverage was enormous—we were totally overwhelmed by the press. The experience was so traumatic that I decided I didn't want to make any more movies or especially go to Cannes.

Since that difficult period, I've learned to deal with the press by ignoring what they say. I feel ready to return to Cannes. More important, I've had to distinguish between two aspects of the career I've chosen: making the film and releasing the film. The artistry of making a movie and the actual work involved is complex and fascinating. All levels of technical and artistic expertise must blend and come together harmoniously.

Unfortunately a film can't release itself, and a certain amount of publicity hype is necessary. But the press has the power to distort and change the way a film is received. At times, exploitation by the press can get so bad it seems crazy to stay in the business.

Obviously, I didn't give up making films, as I threatened, but I did have to come to terms with the press to continue. I had to detach from the negative and focus on the positive. Contending with the pressure of my work is one thing, but having to fight constantly to prove my happiness is ridiculous. I had to learn that what is important is the work and art involved in making a film—not public opinion.

PHOTOGRAPH BY RICHARD AVEDON

Making the Transition from Child's Play to Real Acting

Acting in my first "grown-up" role in the ABC television movie *Wet Gold* during the summer of 1984 gave me confidence for future roles as a young actress. In this movie, I made my own tears for the first time (with the help of some sad music on my Walkman) and had romantic relationships with two different men. It excites me to think about what lies ahead . . . up until now everything has been child's play in comparison.

There is such a distinction between making movies when I was a little girl and now. As a child, I could sit on the cameraman's lap, play with the gaffer's tape; I would look through the camera and eagerly await breaking for lunch. Now my full attention is focused on each scene, the other actors, and the director's instruction—I want to absorb and learn as much as I can.

On the Wet Gold *set.*

GEOFFREY CROFT

Getting playful with Director Rudy Durand on the set of Tilt.

Taking direction from one of the greats: Franco Zeffirelli.

Studying the script with Rudy Durand for Tilt.

As an adult I have to deal with all the emotions and personalities of everyone involved with the film. I have to take responsibility for my actions. I used to be able to say, "But I'm only fourteen." I can't fall back on my age anymore. The days of "Here's Brooke, the little girl . . ." are gone. Now I'm Brooke the young woman. I can't be as frivolous and playful on the set. And I don't dare sit on the cameraman's lap!

When I was younger, I often developed little-girl crushes on crew members while making a film——I guess it's typical adolescent behavior. I

ALAN PAPPÉ

Lots of fun and affection with the crew members from Blue Lagoon.

loved all the hugging and childish flirting I got away with. Often, I'd
sneak up behind one of the electricians and just put my arms around him.
I got such pleasure from all the warmth and affection. It was such a sweet

time in my life. But now I have to stop myself from making any of these gestures or showing overt signs of affection. Everything that I do is taken so seriously. Naturally, men look at me differently now.

Letting go of the childish pleasures is a difficult part of growing up and taking on the adult roles. When you become an adult you are judged by your actions. Consequently, if you want to be treated with respect, you must show respect and act like an adult on all levels.

Meet My Manager: Teri Shields

In many ways, having my mother be my manager works to my advantage. Since I'm her daughter first and her client second, her maternal instincts, the protective aspects of a mother-daughter relationship, have saved me from many pitfalls.

But don't think that she's a "softie"—Teri Shields has the strength and force that every manager should have. She has refused countless offers, protecting me from the hungry money-makers, but, of course, the press never reports that.

In the past, people assumed that I was some sort of "air head" who couldn't think for myself. But the reality is that I've had to make decisions on my own all my life—I've had to choose what I want to do. My mother, like any other manager, presents me with new projects and guides me. She might present three of four different possibilities and then we'll decide together. My biggest problem usually involves scheduling everything because there is so much that I want to do.

I never do anything against my will, in fact, we have a family joke: "I can stop anytime I want to." Saying this to my mother or my Aunt Lila, Mom's associate and my godmother, will always evoke laughter. I love what I do. They know that I'd never want to stop! I'll admit that there are times when I don't feel like working, but I'll push myself and do so anyway—I'm always glad that I did.

I can honestly say that I've never been disappointed with anything that I've worked on. At times, when I can't decide what's best for me, I look to my mother for advice. She has a great intuitive sense and often

MOVIE
STILLS

Alice Sweet Alice, *1975.*

With Eric Roberts in King of the Gypsies, *1977.*

COURTESY COLUMBIA PICTURES

With George Burns in
Just You and Me Kid, *1978.*

COURTESY COLUMBIA PICTURES

With Christopher Atkins in Blue Lagoon, *1979.*

With Martin Hewitt in Endless Love, *1980.*

With Henry and Peter Fonda in Wanda Nevada, *1980.*

Sahara, *1982.*

With Burgess Meredith in Wet Gold, *1984.*

Bob Hope's All American Merry Christmas Show.

Aunt Lila, me, my half-sister Diana, and Mom.

goes with her gut feelings. Mom has helped me build my career gradually. By not going too far in any one direction, she has prevented me from becoming burnt-out or overexposed. I've done just enough work to be very visible. By the time I graduate from Princeton, I will be in the position to proceed full force—all because of the foundation we have built together.

I wouldn't want Teri Shields managing anyone else. I'm really pleased with what I've achieved at this point in my career and on all levels of my life. My mother's love, protection, and wisdom have enabled me to maintain a balance of school, friends, social activities, vacations, and career. My career began at eleven months, when I was the Ivory Soap baby, and it's still going strong, really just beginning, nineteen

FRANCESCO SCAVULLO

One of my very first modeling assignments.

Making my debut as a runway model, age 4.

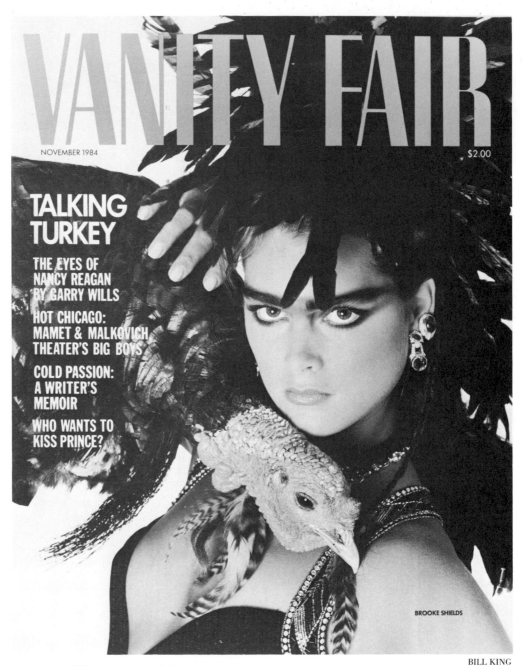

VANITY FAIR

NOVEMBER 1984 $2.00

TALKING TURKEY

THE EYES OF
NANCY REAGAN
BY GARRY WILLS

HOT CHICAGO:
MAMET & MALKOVICH
THEATER'S BIG BOYS

COLD PASSION:
A WRITER'S
MEMOIR

WHO WANTS TO
KISS PRINCE?

BROOKE SHIELDS

BILL KING

*Who says modeling isn't hard work? A real turkey was cast
as my co-star for this November 1984* Vanity Fair *cover.*

years later. It's taken expertise and faultless timing on my manager's part to make it all work.

Making It on My Own

Many people think that I live a charmed life, but the reality is that I work very hard to accomplish what I do. Sometimes I don't feel that I can go the distance. A typical day for me might be classes, a drive into New York City for a fitting or a shoot, and then back to Princeton that same night; all of this with as much studying as possible crammed into every spare moment.

I've been lucky that my mother has been so adept at balancing my schedule that I can do it all, but the final responsibility is mine. Ultimately, I've got to make it on my own. This means complete professionalism at all times; being on time, not complaining when I have a headache—having my energy up for each and every shot or take. In modeling having "the look" is not enough. You've got to know how to work the clothes and to keep your image fresh and clean. There are long hours on your feet in various frozen positions, bright lights that get hot, and lots of people breathing and fussing all over you. You model furs in the middle of the summer and swimsuits on a freezing cold day in the winter. The finished product is glamorous, but the process can be exhausting.

When I have those moments, thinking, "I can't do one more thing!" I remind myself of how badly I want to excel and how much success and achievement mean to me. I've gotten where I am today because I've worked hard to maintain my image, keeping a positive attitude when the going gets tough—determined to continue making it on my own.

❈

FIRST
COVERS

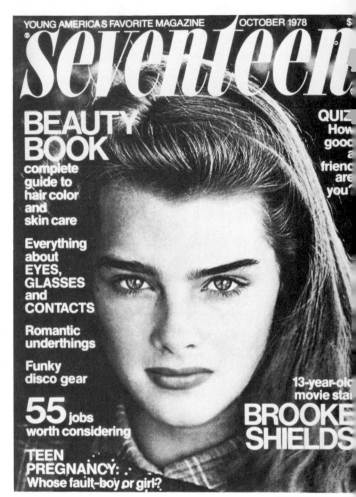

Seventeen, *October 1978*

GEORGE BARKENT

FRANCESCO SCAVULLO

I was the youngest model to grace
Cosmopolitan's *cover, February 1981.*

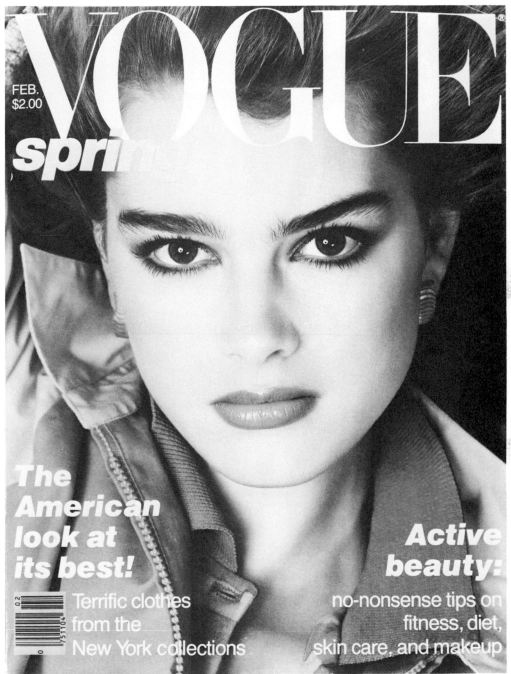

PHOTOGRAPH BY RICHARD AVEDON

February 1980, Vogue.

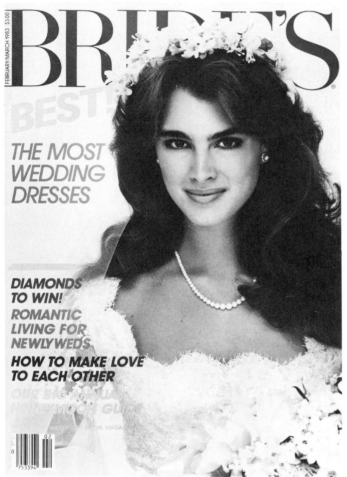

Testing the water . . .
I love to play *bride.*

JACQUES MALIGNON

Bride's, *February/March 1983.*

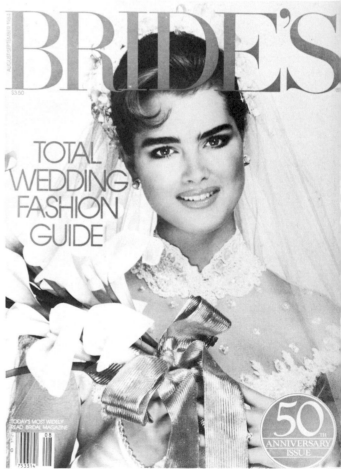

RENATO GRIGNASCHI

Bride's, *August/September 1984.*

Considering Your Options

Many girls are confused about the practical application of their education—how are four years of liberal arts going to prepare them for their career? That's why I think that it's never too early to begin considering how you're going to apply your education to your future. Your college has a wealth of resources at your disposal that will help: guidance counselors, job placement center, exchange programs and internships, and an alumni association—to name just a few.

The first hurdle you need to cross is deciding on a major. Once you've done this you will have the focus and direction for your studies. If you're confused about picking a major, guidance and career counselors are great sounding boards. Sometimes it's hard to know what to choose when you like everything, or when you feel as if you haven't been exposed to enough. A few objective questions and guiding suggestions from a counselor may push the right buttons, helping you make your decision. Speak up—it's your career.

Many schools offer internships and exchange programs (overseas and with other U.S. schools) that can enrich your college experience, and ultimately aid you in making a career decision. What could be better than spending a semester in Greece studying the great tragedies, a semester in France getting hands-on experience speaking French, or a semester in England studying Shakespeare?

When I was in high school, my senior year, I got involved with an internship at the San Diego Zoo. I lived in California for a month and worked in all areas of the zoo and wild animal park. Under the supervision of wild life specialist Joan Embry, I prepared food, fed the animals, and cleaned their cages. I've always loved animals, but working this closely with them gave me a new sensitivity and understanding of their needs and behavior. Although I'm not going to be a zoologist, the internship was a valuable learning experience and something that I'll never forget. And who knows? Maybe I'll do a film in the future where a lion or tiger will be part of the cast—or my leading man!

*Looking after my charges during my high school internship
at the San Diego Zoo.*

ZOOLOGICAL SOCIETY OF SAN DIEGO

Little Viktor really stole my heart.

ZOOLOGICAL SOCIETY OF SAN DIEGO

If you're about to graduate from college, but you are still uncertain about your career—don't panic. Check out job possibilities at the placement office. Often scouts from various corporations will visit schools and conduct interviews. A good job offer could materialize from these interviews, so they are worth arranging.

And don't discount the wisdom of alumni. Read the alumni bulletins and find out what other graduates are doing with their education. Your school could put you in touch with alumni involved in a field that interests you. Talking with past graduates could be helpful with career decisions. They might even take you under their wing and give you a helping hand. At least these "pros" will have some advice and insight about a possible career, and may be a valuable connection to someone else who can help. Believe it or not, you are ready for whatever challenges lie ahead.

If you're planning to go from high school directly into the work force, your top priority should be developing a good track record with your first employer. Being on time and not calling in sick too often is a must. Volunteering for overtime may be a necessary extra to show that you take your job seriously and have potential for advancement. Although this will probably be your first job of many until you find your niche, you'll want to give it your best effort. If or when you do decide to change jobs, get a letter of recommendation before you leave. But you've got to earn that letter—you can't expect a glowing reference if you haven't done your part.

You might want to think about going to night school to develop your technical skills. Improving your typing could mean a promotion from receptionist to secretary. Or if you're unhappy with your present job, but can't afford to quit, learn new skills during your off-hours that will help you get the job you really want. Training is readily available for lab and X-ray technicians, machinists, computer programmers, or any profession. Even though you're not going to college, your education doesn't have to stop.

Some of My Secrets for Success

It's so hard juggling all of it sometimes. I long to be more focused in every aspect of my life. I always want to achieve perfection, but I'm doing so many things at once that I have to settle for almost perfect work at times. I have to make peace with myself, try to relax my standards, and accept that I'm doing the best that I can do.

You can have a million methods for achieving success, but you have to feel secure within yourself to follow through effectively. What if you give something your best shot, but you don't reach your goal, win the prize, or get the job? You certainly don't give up, but there are certain disappointments and limitations that you might have to come to terms with. What's important is that you feel good about yourself no matter what happens. Here are some of the *success secrets* that have helped me along the way as well as contributed to maintaining an inner calm.

Allow yourself the proper time to develop your skills and build your foundation. Ever heard the expression, "Rome wasn't built in a day"? Well, it's true. Get the education first for whatever it is that you want to do. There are no shortcuts to success—only hard work!

Once you're ready to go, *focus*. Don't dissipate your energy—keep it concentrated on the goal you're determined to achieve.

Be realistic. Your goals take time—don't grow impatient because it doesn't happen overnight. Although I began my career when I was eleven months, my first major fashion magazine cover didn't come until I was fourteen, when Patrick Demarchelier shot it for *Bazaar*. Before then, I was too young. I had to be patient until the right time. When I was ten, my girlfriends and I all wanted to be on the cover of *Seventeen*. I waited three years for that dream to come true. At thirteen, I tested for it and got it. Later, I tested for another *Seventeen* cover, but something happened. I've never known what went wrong, but they didn't use the shot. This was a disappointment I had to accept because there was nothing that I could do to change their decision. I could only hope that there would be more covers.

DENIS PIEL

Working with Denis Piel for a September 1983 Vogue *spread.*

DENIS PIEL

The only real mistake you can ever make is giving up too soon. If you quit, you'll never know if you really could have made it. Giving up is automatically losing. Recently I studied very hard for a test and ended up with a B instead of an A—the mistakes I made were stupid and minor. At first my reaction was, "Well, if I studied that hard and only got a B, forget it! I'm not going to study that much anymore." But then I thought, that's giving up. I probably would have done worse if I hadn't been so well prepared. So what I will do is keep striving.

Think positively at all times. I don't ever focus on failure because if I start thinking that I can't do it I won't even try. If I'm going to fail, I'll find out when I do. I'm not going to fall into the trap of dwelling on negative thoughts—it only makes me paranoid and insecure. Appreciate what *you* can do—don't wish you were someone else. It's a terrible waste of energy and an impossibility.

Come to terms with and accept your own level of perfection. Don't judge yourself by other people's standards—you've got to have your own set of rules. Find the niche that you feel comfortable with. Remember that what's right for your girlfriend may not be right for you.

Where I Am Now and Where I See Myself Going

One aspect of my life that is difficult for me to absorb is being a celebrity. During the 1984 summer Olympics, I became aware of how well known I am around the world. My seat was in one of the front rows. As the athletes from different countries paraded by they would begin to chant, "Brooke Shields! Brooke Shields!" Then they would rush over to where I was sitting and offer me their pins and hats. The Japanese were screaming all at once, while the Italians were coming up and giving me kisses. Meanwhile the executives from ABC were asking, "Would you please not go up to them—please just sit down!" But when I didn't stand to receive their pins, hats, and embraces the audience behind me yelled "Boo! Boo! Brooke, go get 'em."

Glamour shots by Demarchelier for French Vogue, September 1983.

DEMARCHELIER

DEMARCHELIER

I must say I felt like the most important person in the world. Here I was, being singled out, even though I had nothing to do with the Olympics. Some of the best athletes in the world were showering me with their love and respect. I was so honored, but I also felt the burden of responsibility that comes with being who I am.

I feel lucky to have come to the realization of what I want to do with my life at an early age. To know that I want to be an actress, that I'm prepared for the dedication it will take, is a very good, very settling feeling. It's distressing to think that some people never know what they really want to do with their lives; they just drift form one thing to another. Since education has always been my primary focus, I have not yet been able to become the kind of actress I want to be. When you're serious about your studies it's a twenty-four hour a day proposition, so for now Princeton is my top priority. I'm majoring in French. So many of the people in the film industry speak French, which serves as a common language for anyone not from the U.S.

Sometimes I find not being able to give myself completely to my acting right now very frustrating. I have to accept the delay because I realize that timing is everything. Once I graduate from Princeton, I am prepared to become the best actress I can be. I don't have any doubts. Although I've already done so much professional work, I'm really just beginning. I feel fresh, invigorated, and ready to go.

I long for a great director and a great project—a real chance as an actress. In so many of my films, there are montage scenes of me walking through the woods, along a beach, in a field. Though this is definitely flattering, I wish just once I would be allowed to look horrible . . . as if I'd just gone through a war and hadn't ever seen a hairbrush. Then the emphasis would have to be on the talent I hope I have.

Just like everyone else, I've always been anxious to grow up. When I imagine the movie roles I'd like to play, I have to face the reality that I've just turned twenty, haven't finished school, haven't been married or had a child—that I'm not mature enough to get the meaty adult parts. I've got the necessary drive, ambition, and desire, but lack the life experiences that enhance artistic expression. As I take on more of an

HORST

*This elegant photograph by Horst, and those following, appeared in
French* Vogue, *October 1984.*

HORST

adult life-style, with the responsibilities that go with it, I know that the necessary experiences will come.

When you're on you own—at school or on the job—view everything that goes on as a chance to enrich yourself, a kind of on-the-job training for your adult life. Good and bad experiences alike will build your character and help prepare you for whatever your future brings.

Time Alone

TIME ALONE means so many things to me. First and foremost, it means privacy. It also means having time to myself to sort out my thoughts, or just to enjoy some quiet activities. I love going to the movies, having dinner at a friend's house, playing with my animals, listening to music in my room—and having some place where I can relax.

Unfortunately, having time to myself and maintaining my privacy are becoming more difficult as I get older. I have obligations and commitments to fulfill and there are so many demands on my time that I'm always busy. It's difficult for me to be out in public without attracting attention. When I start feeling uncomfortable because of all the fuss, I'll do something silly like letting my hair fall into my face or putting on glasses so I won't be recognized. Of course, it never works.

Once I disguised myself with a wig. Then I pulled a hood up over my head, wrapped a scarf around my neck and put on sunglasses. The only part of me that was exposed was my mouth. As I walked down the street a man approached me and said to his friend, "It's *her*—I can tell by the lips." Then someone else came up to me and said, "Brooke, you look awfully funny like that." Needless to say, I felt ridiculous.

There are times when I get tired of being pointed at and stared at—but I have to accept the fact that it goes with the territory. I have to accept the negative aspects of who I am, just as I enjoy the benefits.

Although I have little time to spare, my time alone is very important to me. Everyone needs to learn to enjoy being by themselves, to realize that being alone doesn't have to make you feel lonely. I think that it's a necessary relief to be removed from all of your college activities and friends, even if it's only for an hour. Your time alone is your time to unwind and to do all those frivolous little things you never seem to have time for—something as simple as giving yourself a manicure or just reading a magazine.

Before I can begin to unwind, I need to put my room and my things in order. Maybe I'll just tidy up to get everything organized more efficiently—but I must have neat surroundings if I'm really going to relax. When I clear away the clutter, I feel mentally focused. I feel purged when I take control of the little things in my life that start to bug me because I've let them go for too long—like dirty laundry, scattered class notes, a messy bookbag, my ever-growing pile of papers and clothes that have to be put way.

I love to lock myself away in my room and listen to music. I enjoy Dolly Parton, Phil Collins, Hall and Oates and Joe Cocker. My taste in music depends on my mood. When I feel mellow I listen to Cat Stevens or Reggae; if I feel like "going crazy" Prince and the Pointers always make my mood. And there's always a moment for Michael. A fan sent me a wonderful old tape of accordion music without any way to identify the musician. The music is very emotional and stimulating. It literally brings tears to my eyes. One night, on the set of *Wet Gold,* when we were shooting very late, a group of us gathered in the galley of the boat, played this tape, and one by one began to cry.

Since I have a hard time doing absolutely nothing but listen to music, I usually look though magazines or work on my book of pictures. I have Polaroids from every shoot I've done, and paste them in date books. Or maybe I'll write in the diary I've been keeping for the last eight years. Keeping a journal can give you valuable insights about the special moments in your life and is a great way to work through your feelings, insecurities, and problems.

I consider having a dinner at home with a few good friends to be

Entertaining with friends Cecelie and Lucrecia.

ideal quiet time. It's so much more relaxing than eating out in a restaurant. This sort of intimate evening with friends is a release for me. I love
sharing ideas around a cozy dinner table. After a private evening like
this, I feel relaxed, rejuvenated, and ready to go!

GEOFFREY CROFT

Have you ever seen such a face?

If I had the time, I could spend hours with my pets. I own three cats: Miller, Jeepers, and Boy; two dogs: Jack and Co.; and three horses: Magic, Cobalt, and Erin Starza. My first horse, Magic, was given to me by Peter Fonda. Cobalt was a gift from the late Carl Rosen, and Erin Starza, a beautiful Arabian mare, was a birthday present from Wayne Newton. When I ride my horses or cuddle and play with my other animals

Getting energized with Cobalt and Magic.

There is nothing like the straightforward devotion of my dog Jack.

Feeding a new friend I made while on safari in the summer of '84.

I feel immediate comfort. Pets are so happy when you give them attention, and their enthusiasm makes you feel good about yourself. They are
simple and basically need only love to be content. When I play with my
dog Jack he starts barking and being frisky, as if he's saying, "Wow! This
is great—I love you, Brooke!" The time that I spend with any of my animals fulfills a strong need that I have to love and nurture. Their devotion
is so uncomplicated and so total. I miss them when I'm away, working or
traveling, and I really miss not having them with me at Princeton. Unfortunately, you can't have pets—except maybe goldfish—when you live in
a dorm.

    My favorite activity, for which I make time whenever I can, is going to the movies. I'll bet I have been to every movie theater in the Metropolitan area.

I appreciate seeing good actresses like Meryl Streep, Jessica Lange, Jane Fonda, and JoBeth Williams. I admire actors like Robert de Niro and Kevin Kline who have a style of their own—a quality I want to develop as an actress. While going to a movie is fun and a total escape for me, I'm also studying. I absorb as much as I can about my craft from every movie I see. Going to the movies is very constructive time alone for me.

We all need time away from the hustle-bustle of our daily schedules to sort out our thoughts and feelings. For me, balancing career and studies can be overwhelming at times. Like everyone else, I need a breather—I need to get off by myself just to clear my head and to get some perspective on my life. This is my opportunity to touch base with myself—the opportunity to release any tension and come to terms with myself again. We all need time alone to connect with our feelings. The decisions that you're faced with when you are on your own will benefit from this quiet, thoughtful time.

Sometimes these solitary moments can be painful rather than pleasurable. Maybe there's a problem that needs to be resolved—tension with a friend or family member that must be settled. Whatever the conflict, we have to allow ourselves private time to work it through in our own minds first.

When I have a reflective moment, I am awed by the realization that I am only beginning, that I am standing at the threshold of the real world, on my own, on the verge of coming into my own.

As you take those big steps into the adult world you should always be searching to find new challenges, trying to overstep and go beyond what you've already accomplished. Don't overexert yourself but keep advancing forward, be ready to travel down new avenues and pursue new adventures, even if this means at times that you'll be alone and maybe even a little bit lonely. By making your own decisions concerning all aspects of your life—your physical well-being, career decisions, and personal relationships, and by getting comfortable with yourself and being on your own, you'll be prepared for your wonderful future as a happy, well-adjusted adult in a sometimes crazy world!